Activists, Rebels, and Reformers

Activists, Rebels, and Reformers

Volume 2: G-M

PHILLIS ENGELBERT

Diane Sawinski, Editor

AN IMPRINT OF THE GALE GROUP

DETROIT · NEW YORK · SAN FRANCISCO
LONDON · BOSTON · WOODBRIDGE, CT

Phillis Engelbert

Staff

Diane Sawinski, *U•X•L Senior Editor*
Stacy McConnell and Gerda-Ann Raffaelle, *U•X•L Editors*
Carol DeKane Nagel, *U•X•L Managing Editor*
Thomas L. Romig, *U•X•L Publisher*

Sarah Tomasek, *Permissions Specialist*
Renee McPhail, *Research Assistant to Author*

Dean Dauphinais, *Senior Editor, Imaging and Multimedia Content*
Pamela A. Reed, *Imaging Coordinator*
Robert Duncan, *Imaging Specialist*
Randy Bassett, *Imaging Supervisor*
Barbara J. Yarrow, *Manager, Imaging and Multimedia Content*

Pamela A. E. Galbreath, *Senior Art Director*
Kenn Zorn, *Product Design Manager*

Rita Wimberley, *Senior Buyer*
Dorothy Maki, *Manufacturing Manager*
Evi Seoud, *Assistant Manager, Composition Purchasing and Electronic Prepress*
Mary Beth Trimper, *Manager, Composition and Electronic Prepress*

Linda Mahoney, LM Design, *Typesetting*

Cover photograph of Rigoberta Menchú (with megaphone) reproduced by permission of AP/Wide World Photos. Cover photographs of Mary Harris "Mother" Jones and Frederick Douglass reproduced by permission of the Library of Congress.

Library of Congress Cataloging-in-Publication Data

Engelbert, Phillis.

    Activists, rebels, & reformers / Phillis Engelbert ; Diane Sawinski, editor.

      p. cm.

    Includes bibliographical references and index.

    ISBN 0-7876-4847-7 (set) — ISBN 0-7876-4848-5 (vol. 1) - ISBN 0-7876-4849-3 (vol. 2) —ISBN 0-7876-4850-7 (vol. 3)

    1. Social reformers—Biography—Juvenile literature. 2. Political activists—Biography—Juvenile literature. 3. Dissenters—Biography—Juvenile literature. [1. Reformers. 2. Political activists. 3. Dissenters.] I. Title: Activists, rebels, and reformers. II. Sawinski, Diane M. III. Title.

HN17.5 .E534 2000
303.48'4'0922—dc21
[B]
                                                     00-34365

Printed in the United States of America
10 9 8 7 6 5 4 3 2 1

Contents

Volume 1: A–F

Volume 2: G–M

Volume 3: N–Z

Activists by Cause

Italic numerals indicate volume numbers.

Reader's Guide

Activists, *Rebels, and Reformers* contains biographical sketches of sixty-eight individuals plus seven organizations that have helped shape the course of history. Prominent movers and shakers are covered, as well as lesser-known agitators, from a variety of times and places.

Activists and organizations featured include: Jane Addams, who fought for peace and the rights of women and poor immigrant workers in Chicago at the turn of the twentieth century; Amnesty International, an organization dedicated to upholding human rights around the world and freeing all "prisoners of conscience"; Mohandas Gandhi, who united the citizens of India to peacefully overthrow British rule in the 1940s; and Nelson Mandela, who guided South Africa through a relatively peaceful transition to a multiracial democracy in the 1990s after having spent twenty-five years as a political prisoner. The essays are intended to inform and inspire students, as well as to empower them with the knowledge that ordinary people can make a difference in community and world affairs.

Format

Activists, Rebels, and Reformers is arranged in alphabetical order over three volumes. Each biography is five to ten pages long. Sidebars containing short biographies of associated individuals, descriptions of writings by or about the person or organization in the entry, and other relevant and interesting information highlight the text. More than 120 photographs and illustrations help bring the subject matter to life. Difficult words are defined, cross-references to related entries are made within the text, and a further readings section accompanies each entry. Each volume concludes with a cumulative subject index, providing easy access to the people and movements discussed throughout *Activists, Rebels, and Reformers*.

Special thanks

The author offers most special thanks to Renee McPhail—research czarina, manuscript reader, and extraordinarily good friend. Appreciation is also due to U•X•L editors Diane Sawinski and Gerda-Ann Raffaelle for coordinating the final stages of this project; to University of Michigan Spanish professor Eliana Moya-Raggio and economist Dean Baker of the Washington, D.C.-based Center for Economic and Policy Research for their assistance with select entries; and to the following scholars and activists who suggested entries for inclusion: Rev. Joseph Summers, Ted Sylvester, Ingrid Kock, Kidada Williams, Susan Tachna, and Matt Calvert. Finally, sincere thanks go to Bill Shea and Ryan Patrick Shea—the best husband and son an author could hope for.

Comments and suggestions

We welcome your comments on *Activists, Rebels, and Reformers* as well as your suggestions for entries to be included in future volumes. Please write: Editors, *Activists, Rebels, and Reformers* U•X•L, 27500 Drake Rd., Farmington Hills, MI 48331–3535; call toll-free 1–800–877–4253; fax to 248–699–8097; or send e-mail via http://www.galegroup.com.

Advisory Board

S pecial thanks are due for the invaluable comments and suggestions provided by U•X•L's *Activists, Rebels, and Reformers*
advisors:

- Tracey Easthope, Director of Environmental Health Project, Ecology Center, Ann Arbor, Michigan

- Frances Hasso, Assistant Professor of Sociology and Women's Studies, Oberlin College, Oberlin, Ohio

- Elizabeth James, Librarian, Center for Afroamerican and African Studies, University of Michigan, Ann Arbor, Michigan

- Premilla Nadasen, Assistant Professor of African-American History, Queens College, New York, New York

- Jan Toth-Chernin, Media Specialist, Greenhills School, Ann Arbor, Michigan

Timeline of Events

1818 English Quaker prison reformer **Elizabeth Fry** founds the British Ladies' Society for Promoting the Reformation of Female Prisoners.

1837 Abolitionists **Sarah and Angelina Grimké** undertake a speaking tour of New York State on behalf of the American Anti-Slavery Society.

1837 Attorney and politician **Horace Mann** successfully campaigns to establish a Massachusetts State Board of Education and becomes the board's first secretary. In that position he reforms the state's public school system, making it a model for the rest of the nation.

1847 **Frederick Douglass** begins publishing the antislavery paper *North Star* in Rochester, New York.

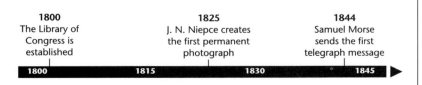

1800
The Library of Congress is established

1825
J. N. Niepce creates the first permanent photograph

1844
Samuel Morse sends the first telegraph message

| 1800 | 1815 | 1830 | 1845 |

1848   **Karl Marx** and Friedrich Engels publish *The Communist Manifesto,* calling on working people to overthrow their governments and establish a communist society.

1848   Women's rights convention is held at Seneca Falls, New York, to discuss women's suffrage and the abolition of slavery.

1850   **Harriet Tubman** makes her first of many journeys into the South to help slaves escape to freedom.

1850   Congress enacts the Fugitive Slave Act, which requires federal marshals to arrest any black person accused of being a runaway slave. This legislation results in the return to the South, and slavery, of many escaped slaves and free blacks in the North and intensifies the battle over slavery.

October 16, 1859   **John Brown** leads a group of twenty-one men on a failed raid of Harpers Ferry armory in Virginia in an attempt to spark an armed rebellion of slaves against their masters.

1865   Slavery is abolished with the passage of the Thirteenth Amendment.

1869   Suffragists **Elizabeth Cady Stanton** and Susan B. Anthony found the National Woman Suffrage Association (NWSA) to press for a constitutional amendment guaranteeing women the right to vote.

1886   Striking workers at Chicago's McCormick Harvesting Machine Company hold a rally in Haymarket Square. Seven police officers are killed by a dynamite bomb detonated at the rally, a crime for which eight union leaders are later convicted despite a lack of evidence. Four of those convicted are eventually hanged.

1850
The Compromise
of 1850 is passed
by Congress

1853
Potato chips
are invented

1861–65
U.S. Civil War

1874
Dominion of Canada
is created

| 1850 | | 1860 | 1870 | 1880 |

1889   Social reformers **Jane Addams** and Ellen G. Starr inaugurate the community center and welfare agency called Hull House in Chicago.

1890   U.S. forces massacre between 150 and 370 Native Americans at Wounded Knee in South Dakota.

1890   The National American Woman Suffrage Association (NAWSA) is formed by the merger of two rival suffrage organizations: the National Woman Suffrage Association and the American Woman Suffrage Association.

1903   Labor leader **Mary Harris "Mother" Jones** leads thousands of youthful textile workers on a 125–mile march from Philadelphia to the New York home of President Theodore Roosevelt to protest child labor.

1911   Mexican revolutionary **Emiliano Zapata** issues his revolutionary manifesto, the *Plan de Alaya,* which advocates the overthrow of the government, the forcible repossession of lands stolen from farmers, and the redistribution of one-third of all plantation lands to peasants.

1912   Workplace safety advocate **Florence Kelley** successfully lobbies for the formation of the United States Children's Bureau, the nation's first child welfare agency.

1913   Feminists **Alice Paul** and Lucy Burns found the radical suffrage organization Congressional Union, which in 1917 becomes part of the National Woman's Party.

1915   Legendary labor leader **Joe Hill** is executed by firing squad in Utah for the alleged murders of a grocery store owner and his son.

1917   **American Friends Service Committee** is founded in Philadelphia to help conscientious objectors (people

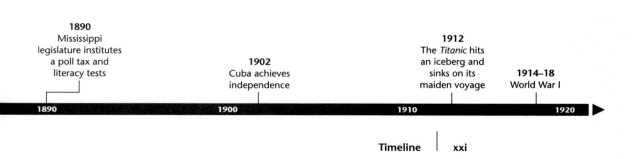

1890
Mississippi legislature institutes a poll tax and literacy tests

1902
Cuba achieves independence

1912
The *Titanic* hits an iceberg and sinks on its maiden voyage

1914–18
World War I

1890   1900   1910   1920

opposed to serving in wars) find alternative ways to serve the global community.

1917 The United States enters World War I (1914–18).

January 1919 Polish revolutionary political leader **Rosa Luxemburg** leads a failed worker rebellion in Berlin, Germany. She is captured and killed by the army.

March 1919 Journalist/activist **John Reed** publishes *Ten Days That Shook the World,* which wins acclaim as the finest eyewitness account of the Russian revolution.

April 1919 Mexican revolutionary **Emiliano Zapata** is assassinated by enemy troops.

December 1919 Russian-American Jewish anarchist **Emma Goldman** is expelled from the United States for her activities protesting U.S. involvement in World War I.

1920 The Nineteenth Amendment is passed, granting women the right to vote.

1925 **A. Philip Randolph** founds the Brotherhood of Sleeping Car Porters, the first black labor union in the United States.

1927–33 Rebel leader **Augusto Cesar Sandino** and his band of guerrilla fighters challenge the U.S. Marines for control of Nicaragua.

1930 **Mohandas Gandhi** leads his fellow Indians on a 240-mile "salt march" to the sea in defiance of British authorities.

1931 **Jane Addams** is awarded the Nobel Peace Prize.

1932 Educator and civil rights activist Myles Horton founds the **Highlander Research and Education Center,** the South's only integrated educational institution at the

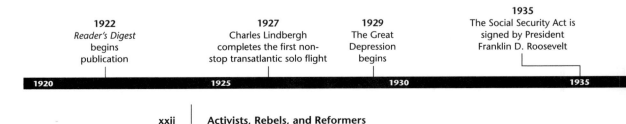

1922
Reader's Digest begins publication

1927
Charles Lindbergh completes the first non-stop transatlantic solo flight

1929
The Great Depression begins

1935
The Social Security Act is signed by President Franklin D. Roosevelt

1920   1925   1930   1935

time, in the Appalachian Mountains near Monteagle, Tennessee.

1935 Peace activist **Dorothy Day** founds the Catholic worker movement in New York.

1940 **Saul Alinsky**, a self-described "professional radical" from Chicago, founds the Industrial Areas Foundation for the training of community organizers.

1947 India achieves independence from Great Britain.

1950 Civil rights activist and performer **Paul Robeson**'s passport is revoked by the U.S. State Department and he is blacklisted by entertainment industry officials for his alleged communist sympathies.

1950 Civil rights activist and educator **Jo Ann Gibson Robinson** takes over as president of the Women's Political Committee (WPC). Under her leadership, the WPC lays the groundwork for the 1955–56 boycott of city buses by African Americans in Montgomery, Alabama.

1954 The Supreme Court, in *Brown v. Board of Education,* declares school segregation unconstitutional.

1955–56 Black residents of Montgomery, Alabama, stage a boycott of city buses, resulting in the racial integration of the buses.

1956 Civil rights activist **Robert F. Williams** takes over the Monroe, North Carolina, chapter of the National Association for the Advancement of Colored People (NAACP; founded in 1909) and arms its members so they can defend local African Americans against the Ku Klux Klan.

1957 Ghana becomes the first African nation to achieve independence from a colonial power and **Kwame Nkrumah** is named its first prime minister.

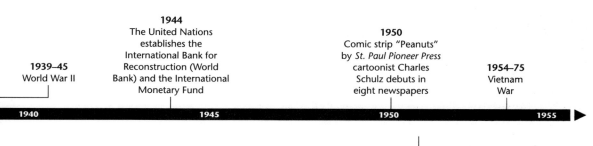

1944
The United Nations establishes the International Bank for Reconstruction (World Bank) and the International Monetary Fund

1950
Comic strip "Peanuts" by *St. Paul Pioneer Press* cartoonist Charles Schulz debuts in eight newspapers

1939–45
World War II

1954–75
Vietnam War

1940   1945   1950   1955

1959 U.S.-backed dictator Fulgencia Batista flees Cuba; Fidel Castro and **Ernesto "Ché" Guevara** lead triumphant rebel troops through the streets of Havana.

1960 The **Student Nonviolent Coordinating Committee** is founded in Raleigh, North Carolina.

1961 Medical doctor and revolutionary **Frantz Fanon** publishes *The Wretched of the Earth,* in which he advocates that colonized people violently overthrow their oppressors.

1961 **Amnesty International** is founded in England by lawyer Peter Benenson with the mission of freeing all "prisoners of conscience."

1962 Peace activist **Tom Hayden** authors "The Port Huron Statement," the political treatise defining the mission of the **Students for a Democratic Society.** The essay calls the American political establishment morally bankrupt and oppressive, and condemns militarism, materialism, and cultural conformity.

1962 Radical civil rights activist **Gloria Richardson** becomes cochair of the Cambridge Nonviolent Action Committee (CNAC). CNAC stages a militant, prolonged fight for the rights of African Americans in Cambridge, Maryland.

May 1963 Young activists of the "children's crusade" march for civil rights in Birmingham, Alabama, and are brutalized by the police.

August 1963 More than 250,000 people participate in the March on Washington for Jobs and Freedom. **Martin Luther King, Jr.,** delivers his "I Have a Dream" speech.

March 1964 Malcolm X forms the black nationalist group Organization of Afro-American Unity (OAAU).

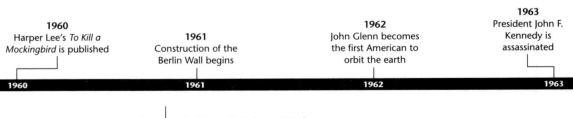

1960
Harper Lee's *To Kill a Mockingbird* is published

1961
Construction of the Berlin Wall begins

1962
John Glenn becomes the first American to orbit the earth

1963
President John F. Kennedy is assassinated

1960   1961   1962   1963

June 1964 One-thousand college-student volunteers descend on Mississippi for the beginning of Freedom Summer. They register voters, run freedom schools, and organize the Mississippi Freedom Democratic Party.

July 1964 President Lyndon B. Johnson signs the Civil Rights Act, thereby outlawing a variety of types of discrimination based on race, color, religion, or national origin.

October 1964 Student activist **Mario Savio** leads the Free Speech Movement on the campus of the University of California at Berkeley.

1965 The National Farm Workers Association, which changes its named to United Farm Workers in April 1966, is founded in Delano, California.

1965 Native American groups in the Pacific Northwest hold "fish-ins" to protest unconstitutional restrictions placed upon their fishing rights by state governments.

1965 Consumer advocate **Ralph Nader** publishes *Unsafe at Any Speed,* in which he criticizes General Motors for marketing the Corvair and other cars that he alleges the company knows to be unsafe.

February 21, 1965 **Malcolm X** is assassinated in Harlem, New York.

August 6, 1965 President Lyndon B. Johnson signs the Voting Rights Act, thereby outlawing all practices used to deny blacks the right to vote and empowering federal registrars to register black voters.

1966 The **Black Panther Party** is founded in Oakland, California.

October 1967 Countercultural activist **Abbie Hoffman** leads 75,000 people in a mass "exorcism of demons" at the

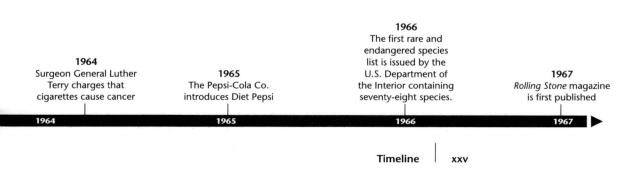

1964
Surgeon General Luther Terry charges that cigarettes cause cancer

1965
The Pepsi-Cola Co. introduces Diet Pepsi

1966
The first rare and endangered species list is issued by the U.S. Department of the Interior containing seventy-eight species.

1967
Rolling Stone magazine is first published

1964   1965   1966   1967

Pentagon in Washington, D.C., in protest of the Vietnam War (1954–75).

April 4, 1968 Martin Luther King, Jr., is assassinated in Memphis, Tennessee.

May 1968 Student activist **Daniel Cohn-Bendit** leads French students in a nationwide revolt.

May 1968 Daniel and Philip Berrigan and seven other peace activists use napalm to burn draft records at the Selective Service office in Catonsville, Maryland, in protest of the Vietnam War (1954–75).

July 1968 The **American Indian Movement** is founded in Minneapolis, Minnesota.

August 1968 Thousands of antiwar and antiracism protesters converge on the Democratic National Convention in Chicago. In what is later described as a "police riot," columns of police beat and tear-gas nonviolent demonstrators.

November 1969–June 1971 Indians of All Tribes occupies Alcatraz Island, San Francisco Bay, California, demanding it be returned to Native Americans.

December 4, 1969 Black Panther Party activists Fred Hampton and Mark Clark are shot to death by police in a predawn raid on their Chicago apartment.

1970 Brazilian educator **Paulo Freire** publishes his most famous book, *Pedagogy of the Oppressed*, in which he outlines a teaching method for illiterate adults that encourages them to participate in the transformation of the society in which they live.

1971 Environmental scientist **Barry Commoner** publishes his best-selling book, *The Closing Circle*, in which he

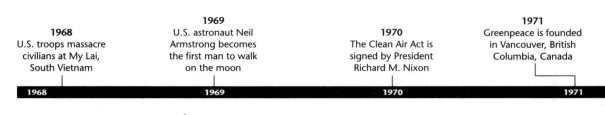

1968
U.S. troops massacre civilians at My Lai, South Vietnam

1969
U.S. astronaut Neil Armstrong becomes the first man to walk on the moon

1970
The Clean Air Act is signed by President Richard M. Nixon

1971
Greenpeace is founded in Vancouver, British Columbia, Canada

| 1968 | 1969 | 1970 | 1971 |

argues that technology has the potential to destroy human society.

1971 **Jesse Jackson** founds PUSH (People United to Serve Humanity) in Chicago.

June 1972 Radical activist **Angela Davis,** in one of the most closely watched trials in history, is acquitted of charges of kidnapping, conspiracy, and murder in connection with the attempted escape of a prisoner in California.

1972–73 Members of the **American Indian Movement** and other Native Americans occupy the village of Wounded Knee on the Pine Ridge Reservation in South Dakota in protest of the corrupt tribal government of chairman Dick Wilson.

1975 Mozambique wins independence from Portugal; **Samora Machel** becomes the new republic's first president.

1976 **Mairead Corrigan and Betty Williams** win the Nobel Peace Prize for their efforts to bring about peace in war-torn Northern Ireland.

1976 Civil rights activist **Unita Blackwell** is elected mayor of Mayersville, Mississippi, a town that had previously denied her the right to vote.

1978 **Lois Gibbs** becomes president of the Love Canal (New York) Homeowners Association, a group organized to fight for the cleanup of hazardous wastes that had been dumped at the site by Hooker Chemical Company in the 1940s.

July 1979 The Sandinista Front for National Liberation (known by the Spanish acronym FSLN, or Sandinistas) topples the U.S.-backed dictatorship in Nicaragua.

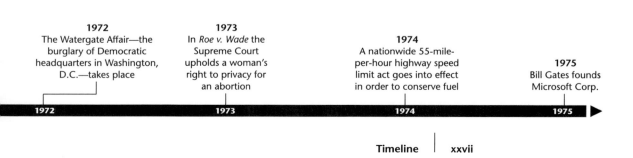

1972
The Watergate Affair—the burglary of Democratic headquarters in Washington, D.C.—takes place

1973
In *Roe v. Wade* the Supreme Court upholds a woman's right to privacy for an abortion

1974
A nationwide 55-mile-per-hour highway speed limit act goes into effect in order to conserve fuel

1975
Bill Gates founds Microsoft Corp.

1972   1973   1974   1975

March 24, 1980 Archbishop **Oscar Romero** of El Salvador, an outspoken critic of the violence committed by the armed forces in his country, is assassinated as he conducts mass.

1982 Egyptian feminist **Nawal El Saadawi** founds the Arab Women's Solidarity Association (AWSA), an international group of Arab women committed to "lifting the veil from the mind" of women.

1982 **Tom Hayden** is elected to the California State Assembly. He serves until 1991, at which time he is elected to the state senate. California's term limit law forced him to give up his state senate seat in 1999.

1983 The Women's Encampment for a Future of Peace and Justice protests nuclear arms at the Seneca Army Depot in Romulus, New York.

1985 The Indigenous Women's Network is founded by women representing three hundred Indian nations at a five-day conference at the Yelm, Washington, home of **Janet McCloud.**

1986 Native American activist **Winona LaDuke** founds the White Earth Land Recovery Project, the goal of which is to buy back or otherwise reclaim former Indian lands.

1988 Indigenous Malaysian **Harrison Ngau** is granted the Right Livelihood Award (considered the alternative Nobel Peace Prize) for his efforts to stop logging in the rainforest of Borneo.

1989 Radical feminist and author **Margaret Randall**'s U.S. citizenship is restored by the Immigration Appeals Board. The Immigration and Naturalization Service had denied Randall's citizenship and tried to deport her from the country in 1985 because her writings

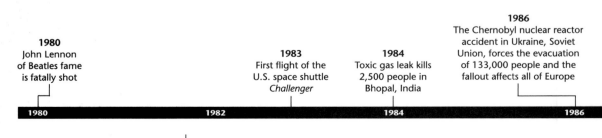

1980
John Lennon
of Beatles fame
is fatally shot

1983
First flight of the
U.S. space shuttle
Challenger

1984
Toxic gas leak kills
2,500 people in
Bhopal, India

1986
The Chernobyl nuclear reactor
accident in Ukraine, Soviet
Union, forces the evacuation
of 133,000 people and the
fallout affects all of Europe

1980   1982   1984   1986

were deemed to "advocate the economic, international and governmental doctrines of world communism."

1990   Israeli lawyer **Felicia Langer** quits her practice of defending Palestinian victims of human rights abuses and leaves the country, stating that justice for Palestinians is impossible in the Israeli military court system.

May 1990   A bomb explodes in the car of environmental activists **Judi Bari** and Darryl Cherney as they drive to a college campus to recruit volunteers for Redwood Summer (a summer-long demonstration against the logging of ancient redwoods). Bari is seriously injured; the case remains unsolved.

1991   **Aung San Suu Kyi** is awarded the Nobel Peace Prize for her efforts to bring democracy to Myanmar (Burma).

1991   **Patricia Ireland** takes over as president of the National Organization for Women (NOW).

1992   **Rigoberta Menchú** receives the Nobel Peace Prize for her work on behalf of social, political, and economic justice for Guatemalan Indians.

1992   Chinese émigré and former political prisoner **Harry Wu** founds the Laogai Foundation in the United States to educate Americans about human rights abuses in China and to advocate for reform.

1993   **Nelson Mandela** and South African President F. W. deKlerk are jointly awarded the Nobel Peace Prize for leading their nation down a nonviolent path toward democracy.

1993   Bangladeshi writer **Taslima Nasrin**'s first novel, *Shame*, is published, leading to calls for her death by Muslim fundamentalists.

1988
Internet virus jams over six thousand military computers

1989
Demolition of the Berlin Wall begins

1991
Operation Desert Storm to end the Persian Gulf War is launched

1994
Major League baseball players strike forces the cancellation of the World Series

1988   1990   1992   1994

1994 **Nelson Mandela** wins the presidency of South Africa in the country's first all-race elections.

1996 The passage of Proposition 209 in California ends that state's policy of affirmative action in government agencies.

1996 **Ralph Nader** and **Winona LaDuke** run for president and vice-president of the United States on the Green Party ticket. (Nader runs again in 2000.)

1997 Chinese pro-democracy activist **Wei Jingsheng** is freed and sent to the United States after spending seventeen years in prison in his native country.

March 4, 1999 Native American activist **Ingrid Washinawatok**, in Colombia to assist the U'wa people in their fight against oil drilling on their land, is killed by rebel soldiers.

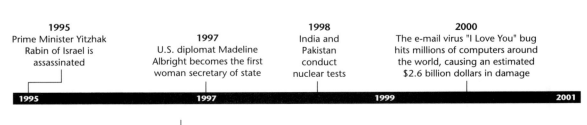

1995
Prime Minister Yitzhak Rabin of Israel is assassinated

1997
U.S. diplomat Madeline Albright becomes the first woman secretary of state

1998
India and Pakistan conduct nuclear tests

2000
The e-mail virus "I Love You" bug hits millions of computers around the world, causing an estimated $2.6 billion dollars in damage

1995   1997   1999   2001

Activists, Rebels, and Reformers

Mohandas K. Gandhi

Born October 2, 1869
Porbandar, Kathiawar, India
Died January 30, 1948
New Delhi, India

Independence activist, spiritual leader, and
nonviolence proponent

Mohandas K. Gandhi was a lawyer by training who found that his true calling was seeking justice in the streets and in the countryside rather than in the courtroom. Gandhi's first battle for equality was fought in South Africa, where he was employed by a law firm. Gandhi refused to accept the indignities of racial discrimination against Indians in South Africa and led a movement to repeal racist laws.

Upon his return to India, Gandhi received the nickname Mahatma, meaning "Great Soul." Gandhi embraced the cause of the poorest of all Indians—the social caste called Untouchables—choosing to don their style of clothing and live among them. Gandhi organized civil disobedience campaigns, which he called "nonviolent noncooperation," to achieve independence from Great Britain. He also advocated unity between Hindus and Muslims. In 1948, at the age of seventy-eight, the man famous for demonstrating the power of nonviolence was himself killed by an assassin's bullets.

Childhood, arranged marriage, and education

Mohandas Karamchand Gandhi was born on October 2, 1869, in the ocean-side city of Porbandar (in the Kathiawar

"Do or die. We shall either free India or die in the attempt."

Mohandas Gandhi

Mohandas K. Gandhi.
Reproduced by permission of AP/Wide World Photos.

peninsula of western India). Gandhi was born into the *Vaisya* caste—the caste comprised of merchants and farmers. (In India's intricate system of castes, or social classes, the *Vaisya* caste is the third-highest of five castes. Not included in the caste system are the impoverished majority of Indians: the Untouchables.) Gandhi's father, Karamchand Gandhi, served as prime minister of four Indian states at various times. His mother, Karamchand Gandhi's fourth wife, was a deeply spiritual woman.

Gandhi was a quiet, shy boy, and an average student. At the age of thirteen his parents arranged a marriage for him to a girl his own age named Kasturba. Although the marriage had been imposed on Gandhi without his consent, he accepted Kasturba as his wife. Gandhi was initially a domineering husband, placing strict controls on his wife's activities, but later came to respect Kasturba for her love and wisdom. The couple eventually had four sons together and an adopted daughter. Mohandas and Kasturba remained married sixty-two years, until Kasturba's death in 1944.

After completing high school Gandhi stated his desire to become a doctor. He was dissuaded from that path, however, by his father, who argued that medicine was beneath the family's caste. Instead, Gandhi chose the more acceptable profession of law. After taking classes for one semester at a local college, Gandhi decided to finish his studies in England. He promised his mother he would abstain from meat and alcohol (as required by his religion, Hinduism) and said goodbye to his wife and baby. Gandhi led a studious and reclusive life in England. He completed his law degree and was accepted to the bar in 1891.

Experiences racism in South Africa

After two years of practicing law in India, with little success, Gandhi accepted a position with a business firm in Durban, Natal province, South Africa. Gandhi experienced his first taste of racism in South Africa soon after his arrival in the country. While traveling by train from Durban to Pretoria, Gandhi was asked to vacate the first-class car in which he was traveling because of the color of his skin. (Prior to the early 1990s, South Africa was ruled by a system of racial segregation called apartheid.) Gandhi refused to leave the car and was tossed off the train at the next station. That incident illuminated for

Gandhi his future path—fighting for justice. Although Gandhi had only planned to stay in South Africa a short time, it would be eighteen years until he would move back to India.

Gandhi set to work writing pamphlets about South Africa's discriminatory laws against Indians—including the prohibition on Indians voting, owning land, or farming; and the requirement that Indians carry passes (identification papers required of all nonwhites in the country) after nine o'clock in the evening. In 1896 Gandhi traveled to India and brought back his wife and two sons. Upon his arrival at the port in South Africa he was beaten by an angry mob. The South African government, partially in response to the negative publicity surrounding the beating, granted Indians the right to vote.

Wins rights for Indians in South Africa

Over the next eight years Gandhi built up a very successful law practice in Durban. Material wealth, however, was not making him content. In 1904 Gandhi established a spiritual center and self-sufficient farming cooperative outside of Durban called the Phoenix Settlement. The settlement was populated by Indians of all religions and all walks of life. Gandhi became deeply religious during that period, meditating and fasting regularly. He shunned material possessions, all forms of violence, and caste differences. He took a vow of chastity in order to further purify himself and demonstrate self-control. He insisted that all members of the community participate in all tasks, such as cleaning, cooking, and tending to the outdoor latrines. Gandhi also published a newspaper dedicated to equal rights for Indians, called *Indian Opinion.*

In 1906 the South African government—intent on driving Indians from the nation—intensified the legal restrictions on Indians. They required that all Indians be fingerprinted and carry passes at all times and placed an excessive tax on Indians coming out of indenture (many Indians had come to South Africa as indentured servants for a period of five years, after which they were free to stay in the country and work or return to India). In response, Gandhi spoke at a mass meeting and convinced some three thousand Indians to pledge noncooperation with the law. Soon thereafter, nearly two thousand Indians burned their passes at a rally in Johannesburg, South Africa. In January 1908 Gandhi was arrested and spent two

Gandhi's Guiding Principles: Satyagraha and Ahimsa

Early in his activist career Gandhi developed the two principles that would guide his words and actions throughout his life: *ahimsa* (ah-HIM-sah) and *satyagraha* (SAHT-yah-grah-hah). Ahimsa is Hindi for nonviolence. Gandhi interpreted the word not only to mean the absence of physical violence, but also the absence of anger, hatred, and all other forms of violence to the soul. His definition encompassed love and respect for all living things.

Satyagraha is a Hindi word coined by Gandhi that literally means "soul force." Satyagraha is defined in many texts as "the force of truth and love." Gandhi continually refined the concept of satyagraha throughout his lifetime. He used it to describe the resistance of injustice through noncooperation and nonviolence, as well as a firm opposition based on truth and love. Gandhi's definition of satyagraha also included the exertion of spiritual power and a cleansing through suffering, as well as the willingness to sacrifice everything in the pursuit of truth.

"Satyagraha is the vindication of truth not by infliction of suffering on the opponent but on one's self," Gandhi wrote. He explained that it was not his goal for his opponents to be crushed, but to be "weaned from error by patience and sympathy."

months in jail—his first jail stint of many throughout his lifetime. In all, he served more than six years in what he called "His Majesty's Hotels."

Despite a series of demonstrations and jailings of Indian activists, things were to get worse before getting better. In 1913 South Africa refused to recognize any marriage not conducted by Christian clergy—thus legally voiding almost all Indian marriages. The government also curtailed all further Indian immigration. Gandhi called for sustained protest marches by Indians throughout all of South Africa. Thousands of Indian miners in the Transvaal (a former province in northeast South Africa) went on strike. When the jails were filled to overflowing, the South African government decided on a compromise. It voided all recently imposed restrictive laws against Indians except the immigration law. Most Indians in South Africa, as well as in India, regarded the compromise as a great victory.

Tours his native India

In 1914, with his work in South Africa done, Gandhi returned to India. The forty-five-year-old leader was greeted by throngs of Indians who came to pay homage to the "Mahatma" (great soul). Although pressured to assume a leadership role in the Indian political community, Gandhi insisted that he was not prepared. Instead he embarked on a year-long train tour of his homeland. He wanted to see how Indians throughout the nation lived and worked.

Gandhi discovered shocking poverty and despair in every city and rural village he visited. The majority of his countrymen worked like slaves while lacking in material needs and self-respect. In some communities English landlords collected high rents and dictated which crops could be grown, while the skeleton-like inhabitants lacked food and water. Gandhi came to understand that there two roots to the problem: British colonialism, which robbed India of its own resources; and the caste system, which robbed people of their dignity. Giving up his tailored English suits for a loincloth and a shawl draped over his shoulders—the clothing of the Untouchables—Gandhi set about to correct those injustices. He established his base of operations in an ashram, or communal home, in the largely Untouchable-populated region near Ahmedabad in the state of Gujarat.

Over the next year Gandhi extracted a few minor concessions from British authorities, such as banning the exportation of Indians as indentured servants, and won rent rebates for the tenants of some greedy landlords. Through Gandhi's intervention, striking textile workers won a pay raise from factory owners. Gandhi came to be revered by the poor and illiterate, and also deeply religious masses of Indians. A second nickname was bestowed upon him: Bapu, which literally means "father," or in Gandhi's case, "father of the nation." Gandhi joined the leadership of the Indian National Congress—the political body advocating independence from Great Britain—to represent the needs of the most impoverished.

Boycotts English cloth; founds "homespun" movement

One of Gandhi's most creative and effective campaigns against British domination was the "homespun" movement.

Gandhi observed that the English system of exporting raw materials from India to England, while importing English goods for sale in India, robbed India's economy while padding England's. Gandhi believed that Indians' refusal to buy English goods—especially clothing—would weaken England's grip over its subjects. He also saw that making clothing in cottage industries would provide work for many unemployed Indians. Besides, Gandhi felt that spinning was a meditative activity that would heighten Indians' sense of spirituality.

Gandhi himself learned the ancient art of spinning thread (which could then be woven into textile) and taught the skill to the members of his ashram (group of disciples). Soon the hum of the spinning wheel could be heard coming from Gandhi's study four hours every day. At Gandhi's urging, Indians throughout the nation shed their imported wear, burning it in huge bonfires, and donned *khadi,* or homespun clothing. The spinning wheel became the unofficial symbol of India's independence movement.

Protests British crackdown on dissent

In early 1919 the British government cracked down on the burgeoning Indian independence movement by passing legislation banning all acts of resistance toward the government. Even possession of writings by Gandhi was grounds for arrest. In response, Gandhi called for a day of prayer and fasting—in effect, a national strike. The action was so successful that virtually all means of transportation and communications throughout the country came to a halt.

In March and April, in the wake of the strike, sporadic marches and demonstrations continued around the nation. Some of those protests turned violent. British forces took the violence to new heights on April 10, when they shot and killed 400 (and wounded another 1,200) unarmed Indians at a rally. The event, named for the northern city in which it occurred, became known as the Amritsar massacre. Disheartened, Gandhi called for an end to the campaign. He undertook a fast that only ended when all protest activities ceased.

The Amritsar massacre caused Gandhi to lose all faith in the British. Until then, he had believed that the British could be reasoned with and that when they finally left India the two nations would part as friends. After the massacre, however, Gandhi told the British authorities in no uncertain terms that it was time for them to leave. Gandhi set forth a program of "progressive nonviolent noncooperation," urging all Indians to continue protesting British rule by boycotting British goods and services and through other peaceful means.

On March 10, 1922, Gandhi was arrested and sentenced to six years in prison for sedition (incitement of rebellion against the government). Two years into his sentence Gandhi contracted appendicitis and had to undergo an operation. The government chose to release him so he could recuperate at a friend's seaside home.

Leads "salt march" to the sea

During the four years following Gandhi's release from prison he avoided active participation in the independence movement. At the end of 1928 he rejoined the leadership of the Indian National Congress and continued the protest campaign. Gandhi sought a way to unify all Indians behind the independence struggle while striking a blow at British domination. He found the answer in salt. Salt, a commodity vital to the lives of Indians, was controlled by the British. It was illegal for Indians to process salt or even to own salt that had not been processed by the government-sponsored industry—despite the presence of salt all along India's immense shoreline.

Gandhi announced a "salt march" to the sea to begin on March 12, 1930. Along with seventy-eight companions, Gandhi set out on the 240-mile march. More than two thousand people from villages along the route swelled the marchers' ranks. On April 6 the group reached the sea. Photographs of the sixty-one-year-old Gandhi holding a palmful of salt, and thus breaking the law, ran the next day on the front pages of newspapers everywhere. Gandhi had captured the imagination of the world.

Ghandi (left) with Indian poet and reformer Sorojini Naidu (1879–1949).
Reproduced by permission of Corbis-Bettmann.

In the days and weeks that followed, Indians swarmed to the beaches to gather salt for sale. The government could not ignore the civil disobedience for long. Police officers swept across the beaches, arresting and briefly imprisoning some sixty thousand Indian men and women.

Seeks independent, unified Hindu-Muslim nation

In the 1930s it was becoming clear to the British colonizers that their time in India was nearing an end. The most pressing issue on the table became the form that an independent India would take. British officials, leaders of religious minorities, and princes of small states argued in favor of dividing India into two or more nations to accommodate the different groups of people. Gandhi was opposed to anything less than a united, independent India. He had long advocated interreligious unity. Although a Hindu by birth, Gandhi also embraced Islam, Christianity, and Judaism.

The question of Indian independence was put on hold as World War II (1939–45) got underway. In 1942 the British government formally offered India independence after the war, with an "opting out" clause for any region that did not wish to be part of a united India. The Indian National Congress rejected the offer. Gandhi called it a "post-dated check on a failing bank" and told the British to "leave India to God or anarchy."

Demanding nothing less than an unconditional British pullout , the Congress launched a final campaign of civil disobedience against the British rulers called the "Quit India" campaign. "Do or die," Gandhi told a crowd in Bombay, India. "We shall either free India or die in the attempt." The entire leadership of the Congress, including Gandhi and Kasturba (who had vowed to speak in her husband's place), was placed under arrest. Kasturba died of a heart attack while in prison. Gandhi contracted malaria soon thereafter and was released in May 1944.

Tries to quell religious violence

While Gandhi and the other leaders had been imprisoned, the split between India's Hindu majority and Muslim minority had widened. Violence had erupted in many places. The dream of a united India seemed more distant than ever. In August 1947 the British left India. Part of India was partitioned off into a Muslim homeland called Pakistan. A depressed Gandhi refused to participate in the celebrations of the independence he had worked so hard to achieve.

A mass migration of Muslims into Pakistan and Hindus (from the area designated Pakistan) into India ensued. Violence between the two groups broke out along the border and spread throughout the land. "If communal strife spreads all over India," Gandhi beseeched the combatants, "what use is our freedom?" He vowed to fast until the violence ended—until death if necessary. Five days into Gandhi's fast, rival leaders laid down their arms and the nation quieted. The weeks of rioting, however, had claimed about one million lives.

Assassinated at prayer meeting

On January 30, 1948, Gandhi prepared for a prayer meeting to be held in the garden of his temporary quarters in New Delhi, India. Despite the insistence of local authorities, Gandhi had refused to let police search attendees for weapons. "If I have to die," declared Gandhi, "I should like to die at the prayer meeting. You are wrong in believing that you can protect me from harm. God is my protector."

As Gandhi walked out to meet his supporters, a young man stepped forward, bowed, then shot Gandhi three times. Gandhi died within moments. It was later learned that the assassin, Nathuram Godse, was an editor of a Hindu extremist magazine. Like many Hindus, Godse had faulted Gandhi for being overly sympathetic to the Muslims.

Following Gandhi's death, his close friend and Nobel-prize-winning poet Rabindranath Tagore stated, "[Gandhi] will always be remembered as one who made his life a lesson for all ages to come." Indeed, as the twentieth century came to a close, Gandhi's life was recalled in countless news stories. *Time* magazine, in its December 31, 1999, edition, named Gandhi as a runner-up to Albert Einstein for its Person of the Century. Einstein, incidentally, was an admirer of Gandhi.

Sources

Books

Chadha, Yogesh. *Gandhi: A Life.* New York: John Wiley & Sons, 1997.

Dalton, Dennis. *Mahatma Gandhi: Nonviolent Power in Action.* New York: Columbia University Press, 1993.

"Gandhi, Mohandas (Karamchand)." *Current Biography.* Edited by Maxine Block. New York: H. W. Wilson Company, 1942, pp. 283–89.

Payne, Robert. *The Life and Death of Mahatma Gandhi.* New York: Konecky & Konecky, 1969.

Severance, John B. *Gandhi: Great Soul.* New York: Clarion Books, 1997.

Sherrow, Victoria. *Mohandas Gandhi: The Power of the Spirit.* Brookfield, CT: The Millbrook Press, 1994.

Articles

McGreary, Johanna. "Runners-up: Mohandas Gandhi." *Time.* December 31, 1999: 188+.

Rushdie, Salman. "Mohandas Gandhi: His Philosophy of Nonviolence and His Passion for Independence Began a Drive for Freedom that Doomed Colonialism." *Time.* April 13, 1998: 128+.

Sudo, Phil. "The Legacy of Gandhi." *Scholastic Update.* April 11, 1997: 12+.

Lois Gibbs

Born June 25, 1951
Grand Island, New York

Environmental activist

Throughout her youth Lois Gibbs had aspired to nothing more than a comfortable life as a homemaker. In 1972 she and her new husband bought a home and began living the American dream. That dream became a nightmare, however, when they learned that their community, called Love Canal, had been built atop a seething cauldron of toxic chemicals. Alarmed by the growing number of unexplained illnesses and birth defects in the neighborhood, Gibbs sought to hold government and industry officials accountable. By 1980, largely due to Gibbs's efforts, the government had purchased every home in the community—thus providing residents the resources to leave.

After Love Canal there was no turning back for Gibbs. She continued her work as an environmental activist and today is director of the Center for Health, Environment, and Justice in Falls Church, Virginia.

Growing up in Grand Island

Gibbs was born Lois Conn on June 25, 1951, in a town just north of Buffalo, New York, called Grand Island. She was

"What we've done here today will look like a *Sesame Street* picnic."

Lois Gibbs after taking two EPA officials hostage in May 1980

203

the third of six children. Her father was a bricklayer, described by Gibbs as rough and abusive, and her mother was a homemaker. Gibbs was a shy child, spending most of her time in the company of her siblings. The thought of speaking before a group was so terrifying to Gibbs that she skipped school on days she was scheduled to give book reports.

Gibbs's education ended with her graduation from high school in 1969. After that she moved to Buffalo, where she worked first as a department store salesclerk and then as a nurse's aide. In Buffalo she met Harry Gibbs, a chemical worker at the local Goodyear plant, and the two were wed.

Marries and moves to Love Canal

In 1972, at the age of twenty-one, Gibbs moved with her husband and infant son, Michael, into the family's newly purchased home. The Gibbses had selected a three-bedroom ranch in a new housing community bordering Niagara Falls called Love Canal. The community was named for a mile-long trench (Love Canal) that had been dug in the 1890s as part of a failed scheme to divert water from the Niagara River for a hydroelectric power plant. The project had been abandoned when its developer, William T. Love, had run out of money.

During her first few years as a homeowner Gibbs happily went about sewing curtains, waxing floors, and cooking meals. "We had a white picket fence, we had a station wagon, we had a healthy child, we had a wood-burning stove, we had cable," Gibbs stated in a 1998 newspaper interview. "We had the whole American dream."

Toxic sludge surfaces after heavy rains

Gibbs's dream did not last for long. It ended with the discovery that the houses of Love Canal had been built on top of a hazardous waste dump. The Gibbses and their neighbors, since moving in, had noticed foul odors in their basements. Some people had developed persistent rashes or coughs. The real evidence surfaced in 1974, however, when heavy rains saturated the earth. Substances welled up from underground, causing metal fences to rust and bushes to die. A young girl's feet were burned when she walked barefoot in the grass; so was the nose of a dog sniffing the grass.

In June 1978 Love Canal's problems were highlighted in a series of articles in the *Niagara Gazette*. The investigative reports listed the chemicals that had been detected in the community and the health problems that were plaguing local residents (among those problems were high incidences of miscarriage and birth defects).

Love Canal's murky history

The *Gazette* reports also outlined the history of Love Canal—that the abandoned trench had been purchased in the 1940s by Hooker Chemical Company. (Hooker, which has since been renamed Occidental Petroleum Corporation, produced pesticides, lye [an ingredient in some soaps], and other chemical products.) For a decade Hooker had used the trench as a dumping ground for its hazardous wastes—more than twenty thousand tons in all. Hooker had then covered the trench and in 1953 sold the land to the local board of education for one dollar.

Despite concerns raised by architects about the underground chemicals, the board of education had a new elementary school—the 99th Street School—built on the site in 1955. Some nine hundred families moved into the area in the years to come, unaware of the toxic waste beneath their feet.

After reading the articles Gibbs became convinced of a connection between the health problems of her son Michael (epilepsy, liver and urinary disorders, and a depressed white-blood-cell count, the last of which made him more susceptible to infections) and his attendance at the 99th Street School. She requested transfers to a different school for her children but her request was denied.

Organizes residents to press for answers

Out of concern for her son's health, the shy and mild-mannered Gibbs began organizing for change. She went door-to-door through her neighborhood, collecting signatures on a petition to close the school. Gibbs found that her neighbors were eager to talk about the contamination and the health problems they believed were caused by the buried chemicals.

In June 1978 Gibbs attended a meeting that the New York State Department of Health had called in response to the *Niagara Gazette* articles. Health officials announced their plan to test houses and soil bordering the canal for toxic chemicals and to test the blood of the people living in those houses. They also promised to install a filtering system on the edges of the canal that would, they claimed, prevent chemicals from passing through. Just to be safe, they warned, people should not eat vegetables from their gardens.

Gibbs and other residents were dissatisfied with the officials' report. They voiced skepticism about the filter, demanded to know whether the 99th Street School was safe, and pressed for a cleanup of the contamination. The officials provided no answers.

School ordered closed

Over the next couple of months Gibbs attended a series of meetings sponsored by government agencies, culminating in an August 2 gathering in the state capital of Albany. The news delivered by State Health Department Commissioner Robert Whalen was a bitter pill for Love Canal residents. "A review of all the available evidence respecting the Love Canal Chemical Waste Landfill," stated Whalen, "has convinced me of a great and immediate peril to the health of the general public residing at or near the site."

Whalen announced that the 99th Street School would be closed. He recommended the evacuation of pregnant women and children under the age of two from the southern edge of the canal area. He also advised all remaining Love Canal residents to stay out of their basements and to keep their children from playing in their yards.

Heads Love Canal Homeowners Association

Following that meeting, residents gathered and formed the Love Canal Homeowners Association (LCHA) to represent the 789 single homes and 250 rental units in the community. The LCHA made its agenda the relocation of all residents who wished to leave the area, the attainment of fair market value for the homes of those people, and the continuing testing and cleanup of the canal. They elected Gibbs to be their president.

Gibbs rapidly grew into her new role. She spoke with reporters, met with health department and Hooker Chemical officials, and even flew to Washington, D.C., to meet with President Jimmy Carter (1924– ; president from 1977–81). By the end of August, under pressure from Gibbs and the LCHA, the federal government agreed to buy the 239 homes closest to the canal site (Gibbs's home was just outside the designated area).

The government at that time declared Love Canal a disaster area, pledging federal funds for a clean up. Gibbs continued pressing for the government to buy all the homes in the community, arguing that the underground contamination did not stop at a street or a backyard fence.

The LCHA also sued Hooker Chemical Company for damages. Hooker consistently denied wrongdoing, claiming they had covered the waste site with a clay liner which, if left undisturbed, would have prevented chemicals from leaking. The LCHA argued that Hooker, in donating the land to the school board (a move Hooker had hoped would absolve it from responsibility), must have foreseen that the clay liner would be punctured. (In fact, the construction of roads, sewers, and buildings, had broken the seal again and again). It was not until 1998 that Hooker paid more than $233 million in an out-of-court settlement to former Love Canal residents and government agencies.

EPA warns of health risks

As the months passed, Gibbs became an increasingly savvy activist. She used the media to shame government officials, whom she accused of sacrificing the health of Love Canal residents in order to protect the nearby Niagara Falls tourism industry, into action. Gibbs coordinated marches, letter-writing campaigns, and visits to government officials by residents. The government continued to move forward slowly, buying out homes only one block at a time.

The waiting game was tough on residents left in the community. While people feared the health risks of staying in their homes, they could not just walk away. Most had their life savings tied up in their homes. They did not want their homes to be repossessed by lending companies, especially when they believed a government buy-out was just around the corner. Some families, like the Gibbses, were housed in motel rooms at government expense while the status of their homes remained in question.

The Love Canal issue exploded in the press when, in December 1978, traces of dioxin were identified in the soil. Dioxin is an extremely toxic chemical, known to cause cancer. It was the most dangerous of the eighty toxic chemicals that had been detected in the Love Canal area. In May 1980 the Environmental Protection Agency (EPA) published a report claiming that Love Canal residents faced an increased risk of numerous health problems, including cancer and birth defects. (An informal survey conducted by the LCHA found that 56 percent of children born at Love Canal had birth defects.)

The evacuation of Love Canal

After the EPA report Gibbs and the LCHA became increasingly impatient with the government's inaction. On May 19, 1980, the LCHA held two EPA officials hostage for five hours at the LCHA headquarters. LCHA representatives demanded that the remaining residents be relocated within a few days. Gibbs threatened that if the government did not take action, "what we've done here today will look like a *Sesame Street* picnic."

President Jimmy Carter responded to the activists' demands two days later, by declaring a health emergency in Love Canal and ordering the evacuation of the remaining seven thousand residents. That October the government paid residents fair market value for the homes they had been forced to leave.

The Love Canal disaster sparked the December 1980 passage of the Comprehensive Environmental Response, Compensation and Liability Act, better known as the Superfund law. The legislation earmarked $1.6 billion in federal funds for the cleanup of contaminated sites around the nation.

"The Love Canal community's fight against the government and a multi-billion-dollar company, Occidental Petroleum Corporation," wrote Gibbs in her 1998 book *Love Canal: The Story Continues,* "demonstrated how ordinary citizens can gain power to win their struggle if they are organized."

The Continuing Saga of Love Canal

In 1988 the New York State Department of Health stated that portions of Love Canal were "as habitable as other areas of Niagara Falls." (The department, however, stopped short of declaring Love Canal "safe.") Two years later some two hundred homes were offered for sale in the northern portion of the neighborhood. The Love Canal Revitalization Agency—the government agency charged with buying the original residents' homes, helping relocate those residents, and revitalizing the abandoned community—renamed the area Black Creek Village.

Gibbs emerged as one of the resettlements' most vocal critics. "There was no way under the sun, I thought, that anyone could convince the public that Love Canal was safe enough to live in," wrote Gibbs in her 1998 book *Love Canal: The Story Continues.* "I was horribly mistaken." Gibbs argued that the measures undertaken to clean up Love Canal were not exhaustive and that the next time the water levels in the community rose the contaminants could resurface.

In December 1999 the Love Canal Revitalization Agency announced that 239 of 240 renovated homes had been sold and that, with its aim accomplished, it was disbanding. Gibbs and other environmentalists continue to sound the alarm about the region. "You can't abandon the people who live there now," Gibbs said of the Revitalization Agency upon hearing its plans to close. "Problems are still being identified."

Moves away and continues career as activist

By the time the Love Canal fight was over, Gibbs had transformed herself from a homemaker into a leader and a fighter. She no longer felt compatible with her husband, and the two divorced.

Gibbs moved with her children to Falls Church, Virginia (just outside of Washington, D.C.), and founded the Citizen's Clearinghouse for Hazardous Waste (CCHW). "We received all these calls from all these different people from across the country," recalled Gibbs in a 1998 interview, "and they were just like me. . . . I realized that I had some sort of responsibility." The missions of the CCHW were to assist people in other communities threatened by hazardous substances and to lobby Congress on environmental matters.

In 1981 Gibbs published an account of the Love Canal battle called *Love Canal: My Story*. The following year Gibbs's activism was featured in the CBS television movie *Lois Gibbs and the Love Canal*.

Founds Center for Health, Environment, and Justice

Over the years the CCHW's purpose expanded to include a broad array of environmental issues. In 1997 the organization reflected those changes in its new name: the Center for Health, Environment, and Justice (CHEJ). The center provides organizational training, advice to grassroots groups fighting contamination, and scientific information. The organization, with Gibbs at the helm, works on issues such as stopping the creation of new hazardous-waste landfills, eliminating dioxin from the environment, protesting the siting of toxic waste facilities near low-income and minority communities, and encouraging recycling. About half of Gibbs's time is spent on the road, working with communities and students. Gibbs is married to coworker and toxicologist Stephen Lester; from that marriage she has two sons.

In 1990 Gibbs was one of six winners (one from each continent) of the first Goldman Environmental Prize. For her accomplishments as a defender of the environment she was awarded $60 thousand. In 1998 Gibbs was selected as one of seven recipients of the Heinz Award. The award, granted by the Heinz Family Foundation, honors (in the words of foundation chairwoman Teresa Heinz) "people who have a passion for excellence and an ability to persevere against all odds."

Sources

Books

Gibbs, Lois (as told to Murray Levine). *Love Canal: My Story.* Albany, NY: State University of New York Press, 1982.

Gibbs, Lois. *Love Canal: The Story Continues . . .* Gabriola Island, BC, Canada: New Society Publishers, 1998.

Krensky, Stephen. *Four against the Odds: The Struggle to Save Our Environment.* New York: Scholastic, Inc., 1992.

Articles

Anderson, Susan Heller. "Chronicle." *New York Times*. April 17, 1990: B10.

Copeland, Libby Ingrid. "Lois Gibbs's Grass-Roots Garden; 20 Years After Love Canal, She's Helping Other Communities Fight Government's Toxic Indifference." *Washington Post*. July 29, 1998: D1+.

"Defenders of the Planet." *Time*. April 23, 1990: 78+.

"Gibbs, Lois." *Current Biography*. September 1999: 33–36.

Gibbs, Lois. "The Legacy of Love Canal." (Op-ed.) *Boston Globe*. August 7, 1998: A25.

Jacobs, Andrew. "Five New Yorkers Win Prizes for Unsung Work." *New York Times*. January 27, 1999: B4.

Pawlak, Hadley. "Love Canal Agency Says Its Work Is Done." *Ann Arbor News*. December 16, 1999: D4.

Sarah Grimké

Born November 26, 1792
Charleston, South Carolina
Died December 23, 1873
Hyde Park, Massachusetts

Angelina Grimké

Born February 20, 1805
Charleston, South Carolina
Died October 26, 1879
Hyde Park, Massachusetts

Abolitionists and women's rights activists

Sarah and Angelina Grimké were among the first women to publicly speak out against slavery in the United States. They were also among the first Americans to advocate that women should receive the same legal and social rights as men.

Sarah Grimké.
Courtesy of the
Library of Congress.

The Grimké sisters were born twelve years apart into a wealthy southern slaveholding family. As young women, first Sarah and then Angelina left their comfortable home in Charleston, South Carolina, to join the antislavery movement in the American North. They became speakers for the American Antislavery Society, touring New York and New England and telling their stories of slavery in the American South. The Grimké sisters were highly visible crusaders at a time when women were largely confined to the sidelines of society and were not allowed to vote, run for office, or go to college.

Aristocratic roots

Sarah and Angelina Grimké were born into a wealthy slaveholding family in Charleston, South Carolina. Sarah was twelve years Angelina's senior; Angelina was the fourteenth and last child of John Faucheraud Grimké and Mary Smith. John Grimké was the chief judge of the South Carolina Supreme Court. Mary Smith came from one of the richest families in the state, and her ancestry included two colonial governors.

The Grimké family lived in a large house in the city of Charleston. Judge Grimké also owned a plantation in Beaufort (on the South Carolina coast) and had hundreds of slaves. While the majority of Grimké's slaves worked at the plantation, a handful were servants in the city residence.

Sarah's childhood

While the education of the boys in the Grimké family was designed to prepare them for professions in such fields as law and medicine, the girls' education was intended to prepare them to be good homemakers and "ladies." Sarah was schooled in basic academics such as reading, writing, a little arithmetic, and French. Lessons in drawing, piano, and voice rounded out her curriculum. Sarah, however, wanted to learn more. Until the age of twelve she spent much of her time studying her older brothers' lessons in mathematics, geography, history, Greek, natural science, and botany.

Sarah was exposed to the cruelty of slavery at an early age. She was four years old when she accidentally witnessed the whipping of a slave woman at the Grimké plantation. It disturbed her so much that she ran away from the house and hid until discovered by her nurse. After that, whenever Sarah heard that a slave was to be punished she shut herself in her room and prayed for mercy for the slave. As was the custom of the times in Charleston, Sarah was assigned a slave girl to be her servant and companion. Sarah became very fond of her slave, Kitty, and treated her as an equal. When the little girl died after just a few years Sarah refused to have another slave take her place.

Sarah's first rebellion

Sarah was just twelve years old when she committed her first act of rebellion against the slave system. Like the other Grimké girls Sarah had taught Bible classes for African American children, slave and free, every Sunday afternoon since she was eight. Sarah asked permission to teach her students how to *read* the Bible and was told by her father that it was against the law to do so. Teaching slaves to read, he told her, might make the slaves restless and defiant. Sarah recalled her response to the situation in an 1827 diary entry:

My great desire in this matter would not be totally suppressed, and I took an almost malicious satisfaction in teaching my little waiting-maid at night, when she was supposed to be occupied in combing and brushing my long locks. The light was put out, the keyhole screened, and flat on our stomachs, before the fire, with the spelling book under our eyes, we defied the laws of South Carolina.

Sarah discovers abolitionist movement

Sarah was almost thirteen when it was time to baptize her new sister, Angelina. Sarah asked to be Angelina's godmother. Although it was an unusual request for a girl Sarah's age, her parents consented. Sarah pledged to cherish, protect, and train her sister, a promise that she spent her life fulfilling.

Sarah spent her teenage years doting on her younger sister and wishing that she could go off to law school like her older brother Thomas. She also led the leisurely life of a young and wealthy Southern belle, with long meals, walks in the garden, shopping, visiting friends, writing letters, horseback riding, and evening strolls through town. Meanwhile, Angelina attended a seminary school for daughters of Charleston's upper class.

In 1819, at age twenty-six, Sarah accompanied her ill father on a trip North to seek medical treatment. Her father died along the way. On her return trip Sarah met a Quaker family who gave her a copy of the writings of a Quaker abolitionist. (The Quakers, or Society of Friends, is a religious organization that stresses nonviolence and simple living.) The pamphlet reinforced Sarah's disdain for slavery. Two years later Sarah left her family and moved north to Philadelphia, Pennsylvania. There she worked and studied with Quakers and eventually converted to their religion.

Angelina joins Sarah in Philadelphia

During her youth Angelina was disturbed by the hypocrisy of the Episcopal Church to which her family belonged. She felt that the church's teachings of brotherly love were inconsistent with the church's endorsement of the cruel institution of slavery. At the age of thirteen Angelina refused confirmation in the Episcopal Church, and at age twenty she converted to Presbyterianism. Angelina taught Bible classes, organized prayer meetings, and urged every church member to speak out against slavery. In 1829, at the age of twenty-four, Angelina joined Sarah in Philadelphia.

By 1831 Angelina had also become a member of the Society of Friends. The Grimké sisters were drawn to the Quaker religion because of its history in the antislavery struggle. American Quakers had opposed slavery since 1688. Quakers had helped establish many of the earliest organizations opposing slavery and assisting free blacks. The Grimké sisters, however, ultimately found the Quakers lacking in principle regarding race relations. They noted, for example, that the blacks who attended Quaker meetings were made to sit in the "Negro benches" at the back of the room.

Angelina began reading abolitionist literature, including William Lloyd Garrison's (1805–1879; see box in **Frederick Douglass** entry) Boston-based weekly newspaper, *The Liberator*. She agreed with Garrison's call for the immediate emancipation (freeing) of all slaves. Angelina attended her first antislavery lecture in February 1835 and a few months later joined the Philadelphia Female Antislavery Society.

Angelina Grimké.
Public Domain.

Sisters train as antislavery speakers

Angelina's antislavery views were made public in the fall of 1835, when a letter she wrote to Garrison was published in *The Liberator*. In her letter Angelina condemned slavery and praised Garrison for his work. The letter caused an uproar in Angelina's home state of South Carolina. Copies of *The Liberator* were burned when they arrived at South Carolina post offices, and a warrant was issued for Angelina's arrest. Angelina's letter also caused a stir among the Quaker elders. Instead of backing off as she was pressured to do, Angelina became strengthened in her convictions. In 1836 she wrote a thirty-six-page antislavery pamphlet titled *Appeal to the Christian Women of the South*.

That same year Angelina was asked to become a speaker for the American Antislavery Society. The Society planned to send speakers all over the North to drum up support for the cause of abolition. Society organizers invited seventy recruits to New York City for training that November—all of them men except Angelina. Angelina brought Sarah along to the training. The next month Sarah wrote her own antislavery pamphlet, *Epistle to the Clergy of the Southern States,* which was published by the American Antislavery Society. In that document she refuted the religious arguments used by southern clergy to support slavery.

Speaking tour of New England

In early 1837 Sarah and Angelina began their speaking tour of New York state. They spoke about their experiences with slavery in the South and stated why they believed slavery should be abolished everywhere. While Southerners were enraged by the sisters' positions on slavery, Northerners were offended by the fact that women were speaking in public to "mixed audiences" of women *and* men. The Grimké sisters were criticized in the press and by the clergy. They were barred from speaking in many churches throughout the North.

In May 1837 the Grimké sisters expanded their tour to all of New England, consistently drawing large crowds. During a five-month period Sarah and Angelina separately visited sixty-seven towns and addressed more than forty thousand people in eighty-eight meetings. In February 1838 Angelina became the first woman to address the state legislature in Massachusetts. For three days she spoke to a packed house. She also presented the legislature with a petition to end slavery, signed by twenty thousand Massachusetts women.

Sisters push for women's rights

The Grimké sisters became celebrated members of the antislavery movement. Their Southern roots and eyewitness accounts of the brutal treatment of slaves gave them a special credibility with northern audiences. The fact that they were women added to their draw, as very few people had ever heard a woman speak in public on any subject.

As the sisters' popularity grew, they began mixing women's rights themes in with their antislavery lectures.

According to the Grimkés, women should be able to vote and make laws. Women should also have the freedom to become doctors, lawyers, and ministers, they argued.

In 1838 Sarah published one of the nation's first statements on women's rights. Her *Letters on the Equality of the Sexes* was published in a newspaper called the *Spectator* and in pamphlet form. In it she argued that nonmales and nonwhites held very similar positions in American society. For example, the law upheld the right for a man to beat his wife or his slave. A husband, or master, also owned all the personal property of his wife or slave. Wages earned by either wife or slave were legally the husband or master's property. Education, Sarah pointed out, was also very limited (if nonexistent) for both women and slaves.

The Grimkés discredited some of the arguments used to justify the oppression of women by pointing out the conditions of slave women. If women were theoretically too weak to work as equals with men, they asked, then why were black women made to work side by side with black men in the fields? They also challenged the common myth that women who had sexual relations outside of marriage would either commit suicide or go mad. If that was the case, they asked, then why were black women able to become pregnant—often as a result of being raped by their masters—then continue to work, give birth, and return to work?

Marriage and motherhood for Angelina

In May 1838 Angelina married Theodore Weld, the abolitionist who had trained her as a speaker in New York. The Society of Friends expelled Angelina for marrying a Presbyterian and Sarah for attending their wedding. Two days after her wedding Angelina and a number of other women gave

Pioneers in the Women's Voting-Rights Movement

Although their activism became tempered over the years, the sisters never lost interest in the causes of equality for women and blacks. In 1868 the Grimké sisters and Theodore Weld served as officers in the Massachusetts Woman Suffrage Association. Two years later the sisters led a group of Hyde Park, Massachusetts, women in an attempt to illegally cast ballots in a local election.

It was not until 1920—forty-seven years after the death of Sarah and forty-one years after the death of Angelina—that the Nineteenth Amendment guaranteed women the right to vote.

speeches to the Philadelphia Antislavery convention. An angry mob threw stones through the windows and later burned the building to the ground.

Angelina, Theodore Weld, and Sarah withdrew from the lecture circuit and moved to Fort Lee, New Jersey. There the sisters compiled newspaper articles on slavery for a book they published in 1839, *American Slavery As It Is: Testimony of a Thousand Witnesses*. The book was an important source for Harriet Beecher Stowe's landmark antislavery novel, *Uncle Tom's Cabin* (1852).

Angelina Grimké and Theodore Weld had three children. Since Angelina was in poor health, Sarah helped raise the children. The Grimké sisters and Weld ran a successful boarding school in New Jersey before relocating to Hyde Park, Massachusetts, near Boston.

Sources

Books

Birney, Catherine H. *Sarah and Angelina Grimké: The First Women Advocates of Abolition and Women's Rights*. Boston: Lee and Shepherd Publishers, 1885.

Ceplair, Larry, ed. *The Public Years of Sarah and Angelina Grimké: Selected Writings 1835–1839*. New York: Columbia University Press, 1989.

Frost, Elizabeth, and Kathryn Cullen-Dupont. *Women's Suffrage in America: An Eyewitness History*. New York: Facts on File, Inc., 1992.

Garraty, John A., and Marc C. Carnes, eds. *American National Biography*. New York: Oxford University Press, 1999.

Lerner, Gerda. *The Grimké Sisters from South Carolina: Rebels against Slavery*. Boston: Houghton Mifflin Company, 1967.

Nies, Judith. *Seven Women: Portraits from the American Radical Tradition*. New York: The Viking Press, 1977.

Emma Goldman

Born June 27, 1869
Kovno, Lithuania
Died May 14, 1940
Toronto, Ontario, Canada

Political activist, lecturer, writer, and nurse

"True emancipation begins neither at the polls or in the courts. It begins in woman's soul."

Emma Goldman in "The Tragedy of Women's Emancipation," in Anarchism and Other Essays, *published in 1911*

Emma Goldman immigrated to the United States in 1885 at the age of sixteen. After working in garment factories in Rochester, New York, and New Haven, Connecticut, Goldman moved to New York City and became a political activist. In 1893 she was charged with inciting a riot and jailed for encouraging unemployed workers to steal bread to feed their families. That was only one of several tussles with the law for Goldman, the most serious occurring during World War I (1914–18), when she was arrested for interfering with the draft.

In 1908 the government stripped Goldman of her American citizenship and in 1919 exiled her to the Soviet Union. Disillusioned with the Soviet revolution, which had taken place two years prior to her arrival, Goldman left the country. She spent the remainder of her years in a permanent state of exile, traveling from one country to another. In the decades since Goldman's death in 1940, her writings on feminism and anarchism (the opposition to all organized forms of government) have retained their popularity.

Emma Goldman.
Reproduced by permission of Corbis Corporation (Bellevue).

Childhood in Lithuania

Goldman was born on June 27, 1869, in the Lithuanian city of Kovno (today called Kaunas). At that time Lithuania was part of the Russian empire—it was incorporated into the newly formed Soviet Union in 1917. Goldman was born into an Orthodox Jewish family. Her parents, Abraham Goldman and Taube Binowitz Zodikow, were already raising two daughters (Helena and Lena) from Zodikow's first marriage.

Goldman and her sisters were treated with anger and indifference by their father, who had only desired sons. Goldman took refuge in her schoolwork and reading. For a time she lived with relatives in Germany, but her treatment there was even worse. Goldman returned home and then moved, with her family, to St. Petersburg, Russia, in 1881. Goldman was forced to quit school—thus abandoning her dreams of becoming a doctor—and work in a factory to contribute to the family's income. She fought off her parents' attempts to impose on her an arranged marriage (their own marriage had been arranged), thus exposing her rebellious nature at an early age.

Immigrates to the United States

In 1885, when Goldman was sixteen years old, she emigrated with her sister Helena to the United States. Their other sister Lena had previously emigrated to Rochester, New York, where she was living with her husband. Emma and Helena lived for a time with Lena and found employment in a garment factory. The Goldmans soon followed their daughters to the United States. Again, Emma felt trapped by monotonous work and threats of an arranged marriage.

In 1887 Goldman fell in love with and married a handsome coworker named Jacob Kershner. It became clear within months, however, that the marriage would not work out. In 1889 the two divorced, and Goldman moved to New Haven, Connecticut. Shamed by the stigma of divorce, Goldman returned to Rochester determined to remarry Kershner and make the marriage work. Things soon fell apart again. The couple divorced once more, and by the year's end Goldman had moved to New York City.

Ideological growth

Goldman jumped into the political activist fray upon her arrival in New York City. By that time she had come to identify with anarchist philosophy. (An anarchist is one who advocates the abolition of all forms of government, as a means of achieving full political liberty.) To Goldman, anarchism was attractive because it promised a society based on justice and reason, and opposed both the centralization of the corporation and the centralization of the state. It also stood for personal liberation and self-fulfillment.

Goldman's politicization had begun during her youth when she read the radical novel *What Is to Be Done?* by Nikolai Chernyshevsky. The heroine of the story was a daring and unconventional woman named Vera Pavlovna, who established a sewing cooperative so she and her friends would not have to toil in a factory for the profits of a wealthy owner.

Goldman had also been profoundly influenced by the 1887 execution of four radical trade unionists involved in the Haymarket Rebellion. The Haymarket Rebellion was an 1886 rally by striking factory workers at Chicago's Haymarket Square, during which a dynamite bomb was thrown at approaching police killing seven officers. The police, in response, fired at random into the crowd. Eight union leaders, known for their antiestablishment politics, were convicted on charges of conspiracy to commit murder despite a lack of evidence linking them to the bomb. Four of those convicted—known as the Haymarket martyrs—were executed.

Learns art of public speaking

In 1889, as a new arrival in the immigrant section of New York's Lower East Side, Goldman met two men—both anarchists—who had a profound influence on her beliefs and life's course: Alexander Berkman and Johann Most. Berkman, a Russian immigrant, was to become Goldman's life-long lover and partner in social causes. Most was editor of the radical newspaper *Freiheit* (Freedom) and a leading anarchist in the United States. He instructed Goldman on the principles of anarchism and techniques for effective public speaking.

Goldman began giving lectures about anarchism around New York City. While she was recognized for her persuasive and eloquent manner of speaking, she won very few converts to the anarchist cause.

The plot to assassinate Carnegie chairman

In 1892 Goldman and Berkman hatched a daring and fateful plot: the assassination of Carnegie Steel tycoon Henry Clay Frick. Frick had directed the violent suppression of a steelworkers' strike at the Homestead steel plant in Pittsburgh, Pennsylvania. Berkman, making what he felt was the ultimate sacrifice to avenge the working people—and one he hoped would inspire workers to take over factories—was to carry out the shooting of Frick. Goldman, afterwards, was to provide the ideological justification for Berkman's action. Berkman fired three shots at Frick but failed to kill him. Berkman was arrested and spent the next fourteen years in prison. Goldman avoided prosecution in the matter.

Jailed for "inciting a riot"

Goldman was forced to reassess her beliefs and strategies in the wake of the doomed assassination plot. She determined that the working class in the United States was not intellectually prepared for the type of revolution that she and Berkman had envisioned. Goldman decided to make justice for unemployed workers her cause. She returned to the lecture circuit, speaking about the right to work and earn a decent living.

In 1893, addressing a rally at Union Square, Goldman quoted religious leader Cardinal Manning: "Demonstrate before the palaces of the rich; demand work. If they do not give you work, demand bread. If they deny you both, take bread. It is your sacred work." For those words Goldman was arrested for "inciting a riot and . . . disbelief in God and government." She was convicted and sentenced to one year in prison.

While behind bars, Goldman received informal nursing training in the prison health. After her release, at the age of twenty-six, she traveled to Vienna, Austria, to earn degrees in nursing and midwifery. She also toured Europe, speaking about political issues in the United States.

The Triangle Shirtwaist Factory Fire

The terrible working conditions of garment industry workers in New York City were made shockingly clear to the world on March 25, 1911. On that date, a fire at the Triangle Shirtwaist Company claimed the lives of 146 workers. Most of the victims were young Jewish or Italian immigrant women and girls.

The fire began on the eighth floor of the building and rapidly spread to the top two floors. Workers were trapped inside burning rooms by doors that had been locked to prevent theft. The fire escape quickly became overloaded and collapsed. The firefighters' ladders, which only extended six stories, were of no use. Left with no other option, many workers leapt to their death from windows eight, nine, or ten stories up.

People throughout the United States were outraged by the incident. One hundred thousand people memorialized the dead workers with a march down Broadway in New York. The tragedy sparked a movement for workplace safety laws, factory fire codes, and child labor laws.

Resumes lecturing

Goldman returned from Europe in 1896 to tend to the poor in New York's slums. Before long she was on the road, lecturing, writing, and organizing workers around the nation. Known by her nickname, "Red Emma," Goldman was a spellbinding speaker (the color red is associated with radical political leanings). She mixed passionate political discourse with humor and sarcasm.

One of Goldman's favorite topics was sexual emancipation. She encouraged women to use contraception in order to free themselves from the worry of unplanned pregnancies. She also lambasted the institution of marriage, charging that it condemned women to lives as "breeders." In 1916 Goldman was imprisoned for her advocacy of birth control (at that time contraception was illegal; it was only legalized in 1936).

Goldman also spoke about workers' rights, the growing trade unionism movement, and anarchism. She decried the unsafe and inhumane conditions in factories, such as those that resulted in loss of life in the 1911 Triangle Shirtwaist factory fire (see box). From 1906 to 1917 Goldman edited and wrote for an anarchist monthly she had founded: *Mother Earth* magazine (Berkman joined her in that endeavor on his release from prison). In 1911 she published a book titled *Anarchism and Other Essays*.

Goldman's inflammatory writing and speaking topics earned her the disdain of many individuals and law enforcement authorities. Despite verbal and physical attacks from vigilantes, and the revocation of her American citizenship in 1908, Goldman would not be silenced.

Opposition to World War I

Goldman was vehemently opposed to U.S. participation in World War I (1914–18). She viewed the war as a battle between powerful parties and of little significance to ordinary citizens. She believed, therefore, that it was inappropriate for ordinary citizens to give their lives in battle. Goldman attempted to dissuade young men who had been drafted from complying with draft orders. For her actions, she was arrested in June 1917 and sentenced to two years in prison. In December 1919, upon her release from prison, Goldman—along with Berkman and 249 radicals of foreign birth—was deported from the country.

Deportation to, and disillusionment with, the Soviet Union

When Goldman arrived in the Soviet Union, the revolutionary communist government was just two years old. Goldman, initially an enthusiastic supporter of the revolution, quickly despaired at what she saw as the centralization of power by Soviet officials. Goldman chronicled her experiences in the Soviet Union in her 1923 book *My Disillusionment in Russia*.

Goldman left the Soviet Union in 1921 and began a sojourn that would last the rest of her life. She lived for periods of time in Sweden, France, and Germany. In 1925 she married an Englishman named James Colton in order to secure British citizenship and a sense of belonging. Fearing that she would become dependent on material and emotional comforts, Goldman decided to move on. Constantly on the go, she lectured and organized throughout Europe and North America.

Supports Republicans in Spanish Civil War

Goldman learned in 1936 that her long-time companion Berkman had committed suicide. Partly in an effort to keep herself from falling into depression, Goldman became involved in what would be the final political undertaking of her life: supporting the Republican forces in the Spanish Civil War.

The Spanish Civil War (1936–39) was a battle between the Republican forces, who were in power, and the opposition Nationalist forces. The two groups occupied opposite ends of the ideological spectrum: the Nationalists were adherents of fascism (a system led by a dictator with complete power, forcibly suppressing opposition, and promoting nationalism and racism), and the Republicans were adherents of anarchism and communism (the latter being a system under which all property is held in common). On the side of the Nationalists were military and church leaders, large landholders, businessmen, and the fascist governments of Italy and Nazi Germany. On the side of the Republicans were urban workers, farm workers, students, much of the educated middle class, and some sixty thousand sympathetic individuals from around the world who comprised the International Brigades. Goldman raised funds for the Republicans, to support their ultimately unsuccessful campaign to keep Spain out of the hands of fascists.

Death in Toronto, burial in Chicago

In February 1940 Goldman was in Toronto, Canada, as part of an international speaking tour about the fascist threat in Spain when she suffered a massive stroke. She died on May 14. The U.S. government permitted Goldman's supporters to transport her body to Chicago's Waldheim Cemetery for burial beside the martyrs of the Haymarket Rebellion.

Goldman's legacy enjoyed a resurgence in popularity in the 1960s and 1970s, when antiestablishment and feminist activists in the United States adopted as their own her messages of defiance and liberation. Goldman's writings became "required reading" in the women's rights movement and activists sported buttons with Goldman's picture and her words: "If I can't dance . . . I don't want to be part of your revolution."

Sources

Books

Falk, Candace Serena. *Love, Anarchy, and Emma Goldman*. New Brunswick, NJ: Rutgers University Press, 1984.

Goldman, Emma. *Living My Life*. 2 Vols. New York: Dover Publications, 1970.

Muggamin, Howard. *The Jewish Americans*. New York: Chelsea House Publishers, 1988.

Wexler, Alice. *Emma Goldman in America*. Boston: Beacon Press, 1984.

Wexler, Alice. *Emma Goldman in Exile: From the Russian Revolution to the Spanish Civil War*. Boston: Beacon Press, 1989.

Articles

Olson, Tod. "Red Emma." *Scholastic Update*. December 8, 1995: 16+.

Pleck, Elizabeth H. "Emma Goldman." *The Reader's Companion to American History*. January 1991: 453+.

Ernesto "Ché" Guevara

Born June 14, 1928
Rosario, Argentina
Died October 9, 1967
La Higuera, Bolivia

Cuban revolutionary and medical doctor

Ernesto "Ché" Guevara was born into a middle-class Argentinian family and was trained as a medical doctor. In his travels through Latin America, Guevara became convinced that the only way to alleviate the suffering of the impoverished masses of people was through armed revolution. His first experience with guerrilla warfare was in Cuba, where, together with Fidel Castro, he led a band of guerrilla fighters in overthrowing the U.S.-backed dictator Fulgencio Batista (1901–1973).

Guevara served as an official in the Cuban government for five years, after which he returned to the life of a guerrilla. He first supported revolutionary fighters in Africa, then organized a guerrilla force in Bolivia. Guevara was captured and executed by a Bolivian army squad in 1967. He continues to be revered worldwide as a revolutionary hero by those who seek justice for the poor.

Childhood in mountain resort

Guevara was born in 1928 to a middle-class family in the city of Rosario, in the east of Argentina. He was the first son

> "Many would call me an adventurer, and I am one of a different sort, one of those that risks his skin to demonstrate what he believes to be true."
>
> *Ché Guevara*

Ernesto "Ché" Guevara.
Reproduced by permission of AP/Wide World Photos.

of Ernesto Guevara Lynch and Celia de la Serna. As a child Guevara was beset by asthma attacks—a condition that would plague him his entire life. To provide a more healthful climate for Guevara, the family moved to a mountain resort community called Alta Gracia. There "Ché," along with his four younger brothers and sisters, spent their childhood.

Guevara, because of his asthma, was tutored at home by his mother rather than attending school. Guevara developed a very close bond with his mother—a woman who influenced him with her radical and nonconformist views. From his family's library Guevara read the controversial works of German economic theorists **Karl Marx** (1818–1883; see entry) and Friedrich Engels (1820–1895; see box in Karl Marx entry), Chilean communist author and poet Pablo Neruda (1904–1973), and Spanish poet-activist Federico Garcia Lorca (1899–1936). Throughout Guevara's life his parents supported him in his revolutionary activities.

Studies medicine

During his teenage years Guevara made up his mind to become a medical doctor. He attended high school at a prestigious institution in the city of Cordoba, interspersing his studies with long bicycle rides through the countryside. After graduating in 1947 he enrolled in medical school at the University of Buenos Aires (the capital of Argentina). Guevara struggled through medical school for four years, despite his poor health and financial difficulties. Before completing his medical degree, however, Guevara grew restless and left school to travel through South America.

Observes South America's social problems

In December 1951 Guevara set off on a motorcycle trek across the Andes with his old friend, biochemist Alberto Granados. The pair traveled through Chile, Peru, Colombia, and Venezuela. They made frequent stops to work at odd jobs, and in that way earned enough money for the next leg of their journey. Touring the continent by motorcycle, Guevara was able to observe the dire poverty in which most people lived.

Guevara and Granados parted ways in Venezuela, where Granados took a job at an institution for people with leprosy (a disease marked by the progressive destruction of tissue). Guevara planned to finish his studies and then rejoin Granados.

Completes medical degree and travels to Guatemala

Guevara returned to Buenos Aires in October 1952 and completed his medical degree in March 1953. He passed the licensing exam and was certified as a medical doctor with a specialty in dermatology (study of the skin).

Guevara then set out for Venezuela, where Granados had a job waiting for him. Guevara only made it as far as La Paz, Bolivia, however, where he met a fellow Argentine named Ricardo Rojo. Rojo convinced Guevara to accompany him to Guatemala, where the government of Jacobo Arbenz Guzmán was instituting extensive social reforms.

Most impressive among Arbenz's social programs was agrarian reform, under which he took over lands belonging to large landowners and foreign corporations for redistribution to landless peasants. Arbenz's policies posed a threat to United States business interests—in particular the largest single landholder in the nation, the Boston-based United Fruit Company. In May 1954 Guevara was in Guatemala to witness the bloody military coup, orchestrated by the U.S. Central Intelligence Agency (CIA), that replaced Arbenz with right-wing dictator Carlos Castillo Armas.

Guevara's associations, like many other young, idealistic, and educated individuals in the country, earned him the label of communist. He sought asylum in the Argentine embassy and later that year escaped to Mexico.

Transformation into a revolutionary

Guevara's experience in Guatemala solidified his commitment to socialism and armed struggle. (Socialism is the belief that the means of production should not be controlled by owners, but by the community as a whole.) Also influential in shaping his ideology were books he had read by revolutionary thinkers **Frantz Fanon** (1925–1961; the intellectual father of armed struggle in Algeria; see entry) and Antonio Gramsci (1891–1937; Italian socialist leader). Guevara agreed, in particular, with Fanon's argument that a just social order could only be brought about by violent revolution.

While in Guatemala Guevara met and fell in love with a Peruvian political leftist named Hilda Gadea Acosta (a leftist is one who favors extensive social reform). Gadea encouraged Guevara's transformation into a political activist. Also in Guatemala, Guevara acquired his nickname "Ché." The name had been bestowed upon him by his friends because of the frequency with which Guevara spoke the word "Ché"—a Spanish term used in Argentina to mean "hey, you."

Meets Fidel Castro in Mexico

Guevara arrived in Mexico City, Mexico, in September 1954 and found work as a physician. Gadea joined him soon thereafter. Although it is not known if the couple legally married, they referred to each other as husband and wife. The couple had a daughter in February 1956.

In the fall of 1955 Guevara had a fateful meeting with brothers Fidel and Raul Castro, Cuban revolutionary leaders in exile. The Castro brothers had spent nearly two years in jail after being captured in a campaign to overthrow U.S.-backed Cuban dictator Fulgencio Batista. After being released in May 1955 as part of a general amnesty (governmental pardon for political offenses), Fidel and Raul had traveled to Mexico. There they assembled an invasion force that would return to Cuba. Guevara agreed to serve as a physician in the Castros' guerrilla army. He joined the rebels in their rigorous training exercises at a secret base outside of Mexico City.

Participates in guerrilla warfare in Cuba

Guevara was one of eighty-two fighters aboard the rickety *Granma* yacht when it reached Cuba on December 2, 1956. All but fifteen of the rebels were killed in their first battle with government troops. Guevara, Fidel and Raul Castro, and the other survivors escaped into the rugged Sierra Maestra mountains in eastern Cuba. There they spent the next two years. They would go down to launch attacks on government posts and then retreat to their mountain hideouts. During that time approximately one thousand Cuban students, workers, and peasants joined the rebel army.

Guevara became noted for both his military and his ideological leadership. He directed his troops "to struggle every day, so that the love for living humanity may be transformed into concrete deeds." On January 30, 1958, the dictator Batista fled the island. Guevara and Fidel Castro led triumphant rebel troops through the streets of Havana, Cuba, the next day. Fidel Castro took over as president and Guevara remained his close advisor.

Works within the new Cuban government

Guevara was named to a series of important posts in the new Cuban government. From November 1959 through February 1961 he was president of the National Bank of Cuba. After that, Guevara was chosen to head the newly created Ministry of Industry.

Guevara was informally labeled Castro's "economic czar." Guevara advised Castro that Cuba should lessen its dependence on growing sugar, an export crop. Guevara believed that the Cuban economy would benefit from the production of diverse crops and from a strengthened manufacturing sector. In addition, Guevara moved the island nation into the Communist bloc by securing an agreement from the Soviet Union to purchase Cuban sugar and to provide other forms of support for Cuba.

Leaves to fight other revolutions

In 1965 Guevara left Cuba to participate in the civil war in the Congo (central African nation renamed Zaire in 1971 and Democratic Republic of the Congo in 1997). The following year, after finding the African revolutionaries' political ideologies to be quite different than his own, Guevara returned to Cuba. In November 1966, after a few months of preparations, Guevara left Cuba for his final campaign in Bolivia—a nation whose citizens were among the poorest in the world.

In Bolivia Guevara attempted to put into practice his theories of social revolution—namely, that a small but committed band of guerrilla fighters could bring down a government. He established a base in the Santa Cruz region of central Bolivia, but was unable to attract many recruits. Much of the time Guevara was incapacitated by asthma attacks.

Fidel Castro, the Cuban Revolution, and the United States

Fidel Castro (1927–) was a young lawyer with a penchant for rousing speeches when he sought to overthrow the corrupt and abusive dictatorship of Fulgencio Batista. After a two-year guerrilla battle, Castro took power in 1959. His first priority was to improve the standard of living for Cuba's poorest citizens. Castro sought to accomplish that by redistributing land and nationalizing (taking government control) of the island's natural resources and industries. He also sent teachers and doctors into the countryside to increase literacy rates and decrease infant mortality rates.

Politicians, businessmen, and wealthy tourists in the United States were outraged at Cuba's economic restructuring. Under Batista, U.S. investments had been protected and investors had turned a large profit. Castro shut down those opportunities. To make matters worse (in the eyes of the U.S. power structure), Cuba had entered into an alliance with the Soviet Union at the height of the Cold War. (The Cold War was the period of tense relations, from 1945 to 1990, between the former Soviet Union and the United States.)

The United States has made several attempts to undermine the Cuban Revolution in the years since Castro took power. For example, U.S. immigration policy (until 1994) encouraged educated and wealthy Cubans to leave the island, thus draining the island of wealth and human resources. And a U.S.-imposed trade embargo has crippled the Cuban economy for four decades.

President Dwight D. Eisenhower (1890–1969), who held office from 1953

Guevara's small band of rebels was captured by Bolivian soldiers on October 8, 1967. The next day, after being interrogated by CIA agents and a Bolivian military squad, Guevara was executed. In his farewell letter to his children (one from his first marriage and four from a second marriage) he wrote, "Always be capable of feeling . . . any injustice committed against anyone anywhere in the world."

Legendary status grows in death

Guevara's early and violent death only served to raise his standing in the eyes of those seeking social change. Guevara became an international icon for social movements of the

Fidel Castro. *Reproduced by permission of Archive Photos.*

John F. Kennedy (1917–1963; president 1961–63), in the unsuccessful invasion by 1,500 Cuban exiles—trained and armed by the Central Intelligence Agency (CIA)—at the Bay of Pigs.

The 1990s—which opened with the breakup of the Soviet Union—saw a gradual thawing of relations between the United States and Cuba. U.S. firms, eager to explore Cuban markets, called for an end to the embargo. And a Reuters poll conducted in the spring of 1999 found that 67 percent of Americans supported ending the embargo. Also in 1999 the White House loosened travel restrictions to Cuba, allowing Americans to fly directly from U.S. cities to Havana, Cuba. As the decade came to a close, proposed legislation aimed at loosening the embargo's provisions was pending in Congress.

through 1961, spearheaded an effort to organize Cuban refugees into a military force to overthrow Castro. That effort was brought to fruition in 1961 by President

1960s and 1970s. He was venerated for his rebellion against corrupt authority and his unceasing fight to improve the lives of the poor.

"[Ché's] ideas, his image, his name, are the banners of the struggle against the injustices of the oppressed and exploited and stir up a passionate interest on the part of students and intellectuals all over the world," wrote Fidel Castro in 1968 in his introduction to *The Diary of Ché Guevara*. "Right in the United States, members of the Negro movement and the radical students, who are constantly increasing in number, have made "Ché's figure their own. In the most combative manifestations of civil rights and against the aggression in

Vietnam, his photographs are wielded as emblems of the struggle. Few times in history, or perhaps never, has a figure, a name, an example, been so universalized with such . . . passionate force."

Remains are reburied in Cuba

For thirty years, Guevara's burial site was unknown. The mystery was solved in 1997 when Guevara's bones were identified as some of those unearthed from a secret mass grave in Bolivia. Other remains in the grave were said to possibly belong to six other guerrilla fighters who were executed with Guevara.

Guevara's remains were flown to Cuba and driven across the island to the city of Santa Clara (the site of a decisive battle in the Cuban revolution) for reburial. In October 1997 hundreds of thousands of people lined the streets of Havana as a motorcade passed by, to pay tribute to the fallen hero of their revolution.

Sources

Books

Castañeda, Jorge G. *Compañero: The Life and Death of Che Guevara*. New York: Alfred A Knopf, 1997.

Cockroft, James D. *The Hispanic Struggle for Social Justice*. New York: Franklin Watts, 1994.

Guevara, Ché. *The Diary of Che Guevara*. New York: Bantam Books, 1968.

Kellner, Douglas. *Ernesto "Ché" Guevara*. New York: Chelsea House Publishers, 1989.

Rius. *Cuba for Beginners*. New York: Pathfinder Press, 1970.

Taibo, Paco Ignacio II. *Guevara, Also Known as Ché*. Translated by Martin Michael Roberts. New York: St. Martin's Press, 1997.

Articles

"Cuban Icon." *U.S. News and World Report*. October 27, 1997: 50.

Dorfman, Ariel. "The Guerrilla: Che Guevara. Though Communism May Have Lost Its Fire, He Remains the Potent Symbol of Rebellion and the Alluring Zeal of Revolution." *Time*. June 14, 1999: 210+.

Padgett, Tim. "Cuba's New Look." *Time*. December 6, 1999: 62–63.

Tom Hayden

Born December 11, 1939
Royal Oak, Michigan

Politician, activist, and writer

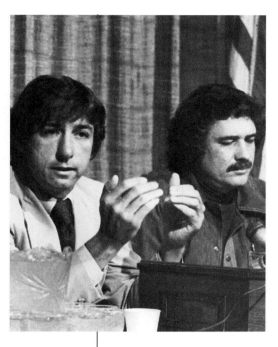

The name Tom Hayden is nearly synonymous with the New Left—the protest movement of the 1960s in which middle-class college students, most of them from urban or suburban areas, opposed the Vietnam War (1954–75), racial discrimination, and the growing economic gulf between rich and poor. Hayden was a leader of one of the most influential groups of the era, the **Students for a Democratic Society** (SDS; see entry), and the author of its famous "The Port Huron Statement."

Hayden participated in civil rights organizing in the American South and worked for economic justice in northern ghettos. He made two highly publicized trips to Vietnam during the Vietnam War to establish contact with the Viet Cong forces (with whom the United States was at war) and was a major organizer of the immense and raucous protests at the 1968 Democratic Party convention in Chicago, Illinois. Hayden was admired by youthful, idealistic activists and vilified by the political establishment.

Later in life Hayden attempted to create change in the legislative arena as an assemblyman and senator in the California government.

"Terror is the disappearance of any line between what is probable and what is only possible."

Tom Hayden in Reunion, *published in 1988*

Tom Hayden (left) with former prisoner of war (POW) Edison Miller.
Reproduced by permission of

Middle-class upbringing

Thomas Emmet Hayden was born on December 11, 1939, to a middle-class family in the Detroit suburb of Royal Oak, Michigan. Hayden's father, an accountant for Chrysler Corporation, was politically conservative. Hayden's parents divorced when Hayden was a child, and his mother, a librarian, raised Tom alone. Hayden developed an interest in journalism while a student at Royal Oak High School. He wrote about issues such as school overcrowding in his school newspaper; his articles and editorials had a decidedly rebellious tone.

Hayden began his college career at the University of Michigan (U-M) in 1957. He majored in journalism, with the hope of someday landing a job as a foreign correspondent. Hayden joined the staff of the student paper the *Michigan Daily* and wrote pieces opposing the school administration's strict rules governing student life.

Political awakening

Several events instrumental in Hayden's political coming-of-age occurred in 1960. Hayden, who had felt alienated by the materialism and conformity of the 1950s, had read the works of Jack Kerouac and other Beat generation writers. (The Beat movement was comprised of young poets, artists, writers, and others who rejected the rigid conformity of mainstream American culture.) Mimicking the protagonist in Kerouac's *On the Road,* Hayden spent his summer vacation hitchhiking to California. There, instead of dropping out of society (as Kerouac's protagonist had done), Hayden immersed himself in the political happenings of the time.

In California Hayden stayed with people helping farm workers in their fight for subsistence wages and habitable housing and spent time with protesters opposing the nuclear weapons research conducted at the Livermore Laboratory. Late in the summer Hayden traveled to Los Angeles, California, to cover the Democratic National Convention for the *Michigan Daily.* There he encountered for the first time people active in the civil rights movement, including **Martin Luther King, Jr.** (1929–1968; see entry), whom he interviewed for the *Daily.*

Hayden returned to the University of Michigan for his senior year and took over as editor of the *Daily.* Under Hayden's influence the paper became a voice of student discontent and civil rights advocacy. Also in his senior year Hayden became involved with Students for a Democratic Society (SDS)—a small, newly formed activist organization that opposed economic injustice and supported civil rights. Al Haber, the U-M student who founded SDS, convinced Hayden to assist with civil rights organizing in the South. Upon graduation from U-M with a bachelor of arts degree in 1961, that was exactly what Hayden did.

Conducts civil rights work in Mississippi

Hayden made his entry into the world of civil rights activism by joining the **Student Nonviolent Coordinating Committee** (SNCC; see entry)—a student civil rights organization that engaged in voter registration activities and nonviolent protests throughout the South. In the fall of 1961 Hayden participated in a voter registration campaign in McComb, Mississippi. In doing so, Hayden knowingly entered a region that was extremely segregated (separated by race, as dictated by law) and hostile toward African Americans and civil rights workers. The handful of SNCC workers already in Mississippi were subjected to frequent beatings and arrests. Hayden himself was beaten by a group of segregationists and arrested while participating in a civil rights march with African American high school students.

"I couldn't get used to the fear growing in me," Hayden wrote about his experience in Mississippi in his 1988 autobiography *Reunion*. "Terror is the disappearance of any line between what is probable and what is only possible. I couldn't tell if the screaming segregationists were going to open fire, or if a car coming down the street was going to swerve and try to run me over. I didn't know how to cope with the raving psychopaths only a few feet away from me."

Takes over reins of Students for a Democratic Society

By 1962, due to the efforts of Haber and Hayden (who had recruited students to the organization during his civil rights activism), SDS had grown to become an umbrella group for student activists nationally. After leaving the South, Hayden returned to U-M to pursue a master's degree in sociology and to serve as president of SDS. Also in 1962 Hayden married a civil rights worker named Sandra "Casey" Cason; the marriage ended in divorce after a few years.

In 1962 Hayden authored the first draft of SDS's political treatise, "The Port Huron Statement." (see box in **Students for a Democratic Society** entry.) The statement spelled out the ideals and principles of SDS—namely the creation of a truly democratic society that reflected the will of communities and individuals—and critiqued the American political establishment.

After completing his master's degree in 1963, Hayden helped found an SDS program called the Economic Research and Action Project (ERAP). The purpose of ERAP was to help poor people in urban areas obtain improvements in housing and city services. Hayden headed up the ERAP office in an all-African American inner-city ward in Newark, New Jersey. Although Hayden and other SDS members spent three years organizing rent strikes (refusal to pay rent until repairs are made) and other tactics to force the hand of negligent landlords and politicians, the all-white student group was never fully accepted by the community. ERAP pulled out of Newark following that city's explosive race riots in 1967.

Opposition to Vietnam War

Hayden's involvement in the movement against the Vietnam War (1954–75) began in 1965. Like many other young people of the day, Hayden was repulsed by the mounting fatalities of both Americans and Vietnamese in the conflict. He visited North Vietnam in 1965 and 1967 to establish a rapport between the American peace movement and the forces with which the United States was at war: the Viet Cong (primarily South Vietnamese communists who were supported by the North Vietnamese army in their efforts to overthrow the U.S.-backed South Vietnamese government). On Hayden's second trip, Viet Cong officials transferred custody to Hayden of three American prisoners of war. The three men, whom Hayden escorted home, were the first American prisoners to be released during the conflict.

After his 1965 visit to Vietnam, Hayden helped organize an SDS antiwar demonstration in Washington, D.C. For the next two years Hayden traveled to college campuses and spoke out against the war. In 1967 Hayden became codirector (along with Rennie Davis) of a national coalition of groups opposing the war called the Mobilization Committee to End the War in Vietnam (nicknamed MOBE). Hayden and other MOBE staffers began planning for massive demonstrations at the 1968 Democratic convention in Chicago.

Organizes protest at Democratic convention in Chicago

In Chicago in the fall of 1968, antiwar protesters joined black power advocates and others to vent their frustration at the political establishment. Tensions were running particularly high because earlier in the year civil rights leader **Martin Luther King, Jr.**, (1929–1968; see entry) and reformist politician Robert F. Kennedy (1925–1968) had both been assassinated. (Hayden had been acquainted with both slain leaders and had served as a pallbearer at Kennedy's funeral.) Kennedy, who had been the top Democratic contender for the presidential nomination until his death, had called for an end to the Vietnam War. Hubert Humphrey, the candidate who was to receive the Democratic Party's nomination at the convention, was less committed to peace.

"The government of the United States is an outlaw institution," Hayden had stated at the start of the protests, "under the control of war criminals."

On the orders of Chicago mayor Richard Daley, columns of police broke up the nonviolent protests outside the convention hall with billy clubs and tear gas. Police indiscriminately beat people, including television and newspaper reporters covering the event. Live television coverage of the convention was interrupted to show the savagery outside the convention hall. Hayden was among the thousands of protesters arrested at the event. The incident was later described in a government report as a "police riot."

Faces conspiracy charges in Chicago Seven trial

Hayden was identified as a ringleader of the Chicago protests along with seven others and charged with conspiracy to

Books by Tom Hayden

Throughout his years of activism, Hayden retained the passion for writing he had developed as a student. Below is a list of books by Hayden, in which he chronicles his experiences in various political movements.

The Other Side, New American Library, 1966. (Co-authored with Staughton Lynd)

Rebellion in Newark: Official Violence and Ghetto Response, Vintage Books, 1967.

Rebellion and Repression: Testimony by Tom Hayden before the National Commission on the Causes and Prevention of Violence, and the House Un-American Activities Committee, World Publishing, 1969.

Trial, Holt, 1970.

The Love of Possession Is a Disease with Them, Holt, 1972.

Vietnam: The Struggle for Peace, 1972–73, Indochina Peace Campaign (Santa Monica), 1973.

The American Future: New Visions beyond Old Frontiers, South End Press, 1980; revised edition published as *The American Future: New Visions beyond the Reagan Administration,* Washington Square Press, 1982.

New Force on the Left, Hoover Institution Press, 1983. (Co-authored with J. H. Bunzel)

Reunion: A Memoir, Random House, 1988.

The Port Huron Statement: The Founding Manifesto of Students for a Democratic Society, Charles Kerr, 1990.

incite a riot. Hayden's co-defendants included **Abbie Hoffman** (see entry) of the countercultural group Yippies (the Youth International Party; a loosely organized group that held gatherings called Festivals of Light rather than meetings), Jerry Rubin of **Students for a Democratic Society** (see entry), Dave Dellinger and Rennie Davis from the National Mobilization to End the War in Vietnam, Bobby Seale of the **Black Panther Party** (see entry), and two other activists named Lee Weiner and John Froines. Seale, who refused to be quiet in the courtroom, was ordered bound and gagged by the judge. A mistrial was declared in his case and he was removed from the defendants' list (the group was thereafter known as the "Chicago Seven").

By refusing to stand when the judge entered the courtroom and employing other antics, the defendants turned the trial into one of the most celebrated pieces of political theatrics in U.S. history. All defendants were eventually acquitted of conspiracy charges. Hayden, Hoffman, Rubin, Dellinger, and Davis were convicted of the lesser charge of "crossing state lines with intent to riot" and sentenced to five years in prison. Their convictions were overturned on appeal two years later, on the grounds that the judge in the trial had antagonized the defense and displayed improper conduct.

Enters arena of electoral politics

After the Chicago protests, Hayden, along with actress/activist Jane Fonda (the pair married in 1973 and divorced in 1988; they had two children), continued agitating for an end to U.S. military involvement in Vietnam. In 1972 Hayden worked on the unsuccessful presidential campaign of liberal candidate Senator George McGovern. Four years later Hayden made his own bid for office, for a California seat in the U.S. Senate. Hayden, whose radical reputation made it difficult for him to garner widespread support, was defeated in the Democratic primary. He surprised observers, however, by managing to capture 40 percent of the primary vote.

Hayden met with success in his second run for office—a seat in the California State Assembly in 1982. In that position Hayden pushed for economic reforms that would benefit poor people, such as restructuring tax codes, placing utilities in public ownership, implementing measures to narrow the income gap between the races and sexes, and passing laws for worker protection and higher wages. Hayden also championed environmental initiatives, such as preserving old-growth redwood forests (see **Judi Bari** entry for details). He railed against nuclear energy (energy derived from the splitting of atomic nuclei) as being unsafe and touted solar energy (energy derived from the sun) as a safe and nonpolluting alternative.

Faces opposition in California senate

Hayden served in the state assembly through 1991 and the following year was elected to the state senate. During his eight years as a state senator (after which he was prevented from running for reelection by term limits) Hayden chaired or was a member of several committees: Energy, Natural Resources and Wildlife, Housing and Urban Affairs, Transportation, and Public Safety.

In the state senate Hayden mainly focused on issues of education and the environment. Conservative lawmakers, however, recalled Hayden's past as a radical activist and worked to spoil his legislative initiatives. A coalition of political conservatives defeated Hayden in his 1994 run for governor of California, and again in his 1997 run for mayor of Los Angeles, California.

After years of political activism, Hayden's political stances softened. In his 1988 memoir *Reunion,* Hayden described himself as a "'born-again' middle American, emotionally charged by my reacceptance in the political mainstream." During his bid for governor he even endorsed the death penalty—a move meant to mollify conservatives but which turned off many of his liberal supporters. After serving eighteen years in the California State legislature, Hayden has been forced out by term limits (laws whereby elected officials can serve only a set number of terms). Hayes was considering running for the Los Angeles City Commission.

In 1993 Hayden married for a third time, to actress Barbara Williams, in a ceremony conducted by a Buddhist priest.

Sources

Books

Anderson, Terry H. *The Movement and the Sixties: Protest in America from Greensboro to Wounded Knee.* New York: Oxford University Press, 1995.

Gitlin, Todd. *The Sixties: Years of Hope, Days of Rage.* New York: Bantam Books, 1987.

Hamilton, Neil A. *The ABC-CLIO Companion to the 1960s Counterculture in America.* Santa Barbara, CA: ABC-CLIO, 1997, pp. 140–43.

Hayden, Tom. *Reunion: A Memoir.* New York: Random House, 1988.

McGuire, Willliam, and Leslie Wheeler. *American Social Leaders.* Santa Barbara, CA: ABC-CLIO, 1993, pp. 223–24.

Articles

Ayres, B. Drummond, Jr. "System Catches Up with Tom Hayden." *New York Times.* August 27, 2000: A20. national edition.

"Hayden Abandons Assembly Bid." *Los Angeles Business Journal.* November 14, 1999: 73.

Highlander Research and Education Center

Founded 1932
New Market, Tennessee

Training center for social justice activists

The Highlander Research and Education Center—formerly called the Highlander Folk School—is a community adult education center nestled in the mountains east of Knoxville, Tennessee. Highlander serves as a training facility for activist organizations and labor unions and promotes civil rights and environmental protection.

The Highlander Center was founded in 1932 by Myles Horton (1905–1990; see box in **Paulo Freire** entry), an educator, and civil rights and labor activist. Horton, who directed the center for nearly sixty years, held the philosophy that every individual possesses the power to improve his or her own conditions and make the world a better place for all.

Highlander was racially integrated from its inception, making it a one-of-a-kind institution in the pre-civil rights era American South. Because Highlander defied Jim Crow laws (rules defining the separation of races on every level of society), it came under fire from racist groups and conservative lawmakers in the 1950s and 1960s.

Highlander has played an important role in the development of the American labor and civil rights movements.

Highlander's early years

The Highlander Folk School was established by Myles Horton in 1932 in the Appalachian Mountains near Monteagle, Tennessee. Dr. Lillian Johnson, a leader in the movement for women's voting rights and a member of a wealthy Memphis, Tennessee, banking family, donated the school building and land on which it sat. The name "Highlander" was a nickname by which residents of the Appalachian Mountains were known.

One of Highlander's original missions was to provide leadership training for union activists and oppressed workers from Appalachia—particularly coal miners, timber cutters, and textile workers. The school offered workshops, cosponsored by the Congress of Industrial Organization (CIO; a federation of labor organizations that later merged with the American Federation of Labor), on labor history, economics, workers' rights, race relations, and organizing strategies. The sessions were informal and directed by students.

Serves the surrounding community

Highlander also served as a school for adults from the surrounding impoverished region and a community center. Four nights a week there were classes on psychology, current events, geography, and political science. Highlander offered an extensive lending library, square dances, free music lessons for children, a nursery school, a community cannery, and a quilting cooperative.

Highlander developed a strong musical tradition, as well, and popularized numerous protest songs and spirituals. Zilphia Johnson, whom Myles Horton married in 1935 (she then became Zilphia Horton), coordinated the school's music and drama programs and was the school's community relations director. Zilphia Horton, together with folk musicians Pete Seeger, Frank Hamilton, and Guy Carawan, is credited for adapting an old Negro spiritual into "We Shall Overcome"—the song that became the anthem of the civil rights movement.

Moves into civil rights arena

In the 1950s Highlander switched its focus from labor education to civil rights and race relations—in particular the desegregation of southern public schools. "The next great problem is not the problem of conquering poverty, but conquering meanness, prejudice, and tradition," wrote the Highlander board at its April 1953 meeting. "Highlander could become the place in which this is studied, a place where one could learn the art of practice and methods of brotherhood. The new emphasis at Highlander should be on the desegregation of the public schools in the South."

Throughout the 1950s Highlander helped thousands of African Americans and whites develop the skills and confidence needed to challenge segregation laws. Many of the people trained at Highlander, such as **Martin Luther King, Jr.,** (1929–1968; see entry), Rosa Parks (1913– ; see box in this entry), Fannie Lou Hamer (1917–1977; see box in **Ella Baker** entry), and John Lewis (1940–; see box in **Student Nonviolent Coordinating Committee** entry), went on to play key roles in the civil rights movement.

Highlander's civil rights work involved workshops on the philosophy and practice of nonviolence for racially mixed groups of students and activists. In order to expand the membership base of the civil rights movement, Highlander developed a model of adult education called the "citizenship school."

Citizenship schools

Citizenship schools were classes for adults that covered such basic skills as reading, writing, and math. Students were also taught how to fill out voter registration applications and drivers' license applications, and how to write checks and money orders. The schools were intended not only to boost the voter registration of African Americans but to prepare students to participate more fully in the mainstream of American life. (African Americans were kept from voting throughout the South until 1965 by a variety of legal means, as well as the threat of physical violence. If prospective African American voters could not read and write, they had no chance of passing the "literacy test" that was required for voting.)

"We weren't thinking of it primarily as a literacy program," Horton wrote regarding the citizenship schools in his autobiography, "because teaching people to read and write was only one step toward their becoming citizens and social

Rosa Parks Puts Highlander Ideals Into Practice

Rosa Parks (1913-) made her legendary refusal to give up her seat on a Montgomery, Alabama, city bus on December 1, 1955. Just seven weeks earlier, Parks—the secretary of the Montgomery branch of the National Association for the Advancement of Colored People (NAACP)—had attended a training session at the Highlander Folk School.

"I found out for the first time in my adult life," Parks stated in the video documentary *Eyes on the Prize* about her experience at Highlander, "that this could be a unified society, that there was such a thing as people of differing races and backgrounds meeting together in workshops and living together in peace and harmony. It was a place I was very reluctant to leave."

Parks's courageous stand on the bus, and her subsequent arrest, sparked a 382-day bus boycott that led to the desegregation of Montgomery buses and inspired African Americans in many other southern cities to challenge segregation on their buses (see entry on **Jo Ann Gibson Robinson**).

Parks was born in Tuskegee, Alabama, in 1913. When she was two years old her parents separated, and she moved to Montgomery with her mother and brother. Parks was schooled at home until the age of eleven, after which she attended the all-black Montgomery Industrial School for Girls. Parks then studied for a brief time at Alabama State University.

Parks's 1955 bus protest was not her first instance of civil rights activism. In the 1930s she had worked to free the Scottsboro Boys—nine young African American men falsely accused of raping two white women. And in 1944 Parks had

activists. The immediate goal was getting the right to vote. Becoming literate was only a part of a larger process. . . . Our objective was to help them understand that they could both play a role at home and help change the world."

Highlander sponsored citizenship schools not only at its Monteagle headquarters but in numerous locations throughout the South. Horton hired Septima Clark (1898–1987), a schoolteacher from Charleston, South Carolina, who had been fired because of her involvement in the NAACP, to direct Highlander's citizenship school program. Clark set up scores of citizenship schools, with local people

Rosa Parks on a Montgomery, Alabama, bus in 1956. She defied Jim Crow laws by taking a seat in the front of the bus. *Reproduced by permission of Corbis Corporation.*

captured national attention, she was working as a seamstress at Fair Department Store. Her activism, however, cost Parks her job.

In 1957 Parks and her husband, Raymond Parks, moved to Detroit, Michigan, to escape the publicity and to find employment. There she created the Rosa and Raymond Parks Institute for Self Development—a nonprofit organization that promotes racial and social harmony. Parks still resides in Detroit and remains active in community organizations and youth programs. In 1999 she was awarded the Congressional Gold Medal, the highest civilian honor given by Congress.

refused to move to the back of a city bus, which resulted in her being forced off the bus. In 1955, when Parks's bus protest

serving as teachers. Classes were held in private homes, country stores, beauty parlors, and under trees.

Citizenship school alumni make waves

Many citizenship school graduates went on to become civil rights organizers. Rosa Parks, for example, made her stand on a Montgomery, Alabama, bus just seven weeks after returning from Highlander. Fannie Lou Hamer, spokesperson for the Mississippi Freedom Democratic Party, also went through a Highlander citizenship school. And Esau Jenkins, a farmer, bus driver, and father of seven from Johns Island, South Carolina, spearheaded a school desegregation campaign following his attendance at a citizenship school.

The citizenship schools were widely hailed as the nation's most successful mass-literacy program. Andrew Young (1921–)—civil rights activist and, later, U.S. ambassador to the United Nations and mayor of Atlanta—remarked that the citizenship schools had laid the foundation for the entire civil rights movement.

Highlander comes under attack

Because Highlander was an integrated institution in defiance of Jim Crow laws, it constantly came under fire from racist groups and conservative lawmakers. The Ku Klux Klan (a white supremacist organization) paid many visits to the small school, vandalizing the property, threatening the staff, and spray painting "KKK was here."

In 1957 Senator James O. Eastland, the notorious segregationist from Mississippi and chair of the Senate Internal Security subcommittee, together with Arkansas attorney general Bruce Bennett, embarked on a mission to shut down Highlander. Eastland and Bennett accused Horton of being a communist (communism is the theory of social organization based on the holding of all property in common). While Horton admitted to welcoming communists as he did all interested parties, he denied embracing communism himself. Eastland and Bennett also charged that Highlander was operating in violation of segregation laws.

The Internal Revenue Service punished Highlander for its violation of segregation laws by withdrawing Highlander's tax-exempt status in 1957. Prosecutors from Tennessee, at Eastland's urging, then fabricated charges that Highlander was selling alcohol without a license. In 1960 the Tennessee courts ordered that Highlander close its doors. Horton left Monteagle and the next year reopened the school in Knoxville, Tennessee, naming it the Highlander Research and Education Center.

Highlander moves to new location

In 1972 Highlander moved to its present location, a one hundred-acre farm outside of New Market, Tennessee, overlooking Great Smoky Mountains National Park. In the 1970s Highlander shifted its focus to environmental concerns (such as nuclear waste and strip mining) and issues of economic justice.

Today Highlander continues to operate as an educational center for individuals and grassroots organizations. Highlander embraces a broad range of social causes, including civil rights, economic democracy, environmental justice, community empowerment, labor rights, and women's rights.

"Today the Highlander Research and Education Center remains committed to working with grassroots leaders and community groups to help bring about social change through collective action," reads a 1999 Highlander brochure. "Through its efforts to assist societal transformation, Highlander serves as a safe place where people can talk freely about their lives and build bridges of solidarity for social change with others."

Sources

Books

Bledsoe, Thomas. *Or We'll All Hang Separately: The Highlander Idea.* Boston: Beacon Press, 1969.

Egerton, John. *Speak Now against the Day: The Generation before the Civil Rights Movement in the South.* New York: Alfred A. Knopf, 1994.

Horton, Myles, with Judith Kohl and Herbert Kohl. *The Long Haul: An Autobiography.* New York: Doubleday, 1990.

Langston, Donna. "The Women of Highlander." In *Women in the Civil Rights Movement: Trailblazers and Torchbearers, 1941–1965,* edited by Vicki L Crawford, Jacqueline Anne Rouse, and Barbara Woods. Brooklyn, NY: Carlson Publishing Inc., 1990, pp. 145–65.

Wigginton, Eliot. *Refuse to Stand Silently By: An Oral History of Grass Roots Social Activism in America, 1921–1964.* New York: Doubleday, 1991.

Articles

Miller, Geralda. "Parks Gets Congressional Gold Medal." *Ann Arbor News.* November 29, 1999: C4.

"Myles Horton" Obituary. *The Nation.* February 19, 1990: 224.

Web Sites

Highlander Center: Historical and Philosophical Tour. [Online] Available http://www.people.cornell.edu/pages/hlh2/tour.htm (accessed March 17, 2000).

Other Sources

"1998–1999 Annual Report." Highlander Research and Education Center. New Market, Tennessee.

Eyes on the Prize: America's Civil Rights Years. Boston: Blackside, Inc., 1986. Videocassettes; six episodes.

You've Got to Move. New York: First Run/Icarus Films, 1985. Videocassette.

Joe Hill

Born October 7, 1879
Gävle, Sweden
Died November 19, 1915
Salt Lake City, Utah

Labor organizer, songwriter, musician, and author

Joe Hill became a member of the struggling migrant working class in America upon emigrating from his native Sweden in 1902. He joined a burgeoning radical labor organization—the Industrial Workers of the World (IWW)—which sought to form one big union of all the world's "producers." Hill traveled around the United States, mostly on the West Coast, organizing underpaid and overworked workers. He urged them to stand up to their bosses with demonstrations, strikes, and—if all else failed—sabotage and violence.

Hill wrote articles for the IWW newspaper and composed folksongs for the IWW's "Little Red Songbook." His songs were memorized and passed along by workers everywhere. He is credited with turning the labor movement into a "singing movement." In 1915 he was executed by firing squad after being convicted, on circumstantial evidence, of murdering a grocery store owner and his son.

Early years in Sweden

Joe Hill was born Joel Emanuel Hägglund (pronounced HEG-lund) in Gävle, Sweden. Gävle is a small port city some

"I will die like a true blue rebel. Don't waste any time in mourning. *Organize.*"

The final message sent by Joe Hill to a friend before his execution by firing squad.

Joe Hill.
Reproduced by permission of Corbis Corporation (Bellevue).

251

one hundred miles north of the capital of Stockholm. Hill was the third of nine children, three of whom died in infancy. The family, though poor, was able to meet its basic needs. Both of Hill's parents valued musical education, and Hill learned to play several instruments and write songs in his youth.

Hill's father, a conductor on the railroad, died in a work-related accident when Hill was eight years old. With nothing but their mother's small widow's pension to support the large family, Hill and his siblings were forced to find work. Hill helped his mother wash and iron other people's laundry and did odd jobs after school. He quit school at the age of fourteen to work full time at a rope factory. He then found employment on a steamship, where his job was to keep the fire going in the ship's boiler.

At the age of twenty Hill fell ill with tuberculosis—an infectious disease that usually affects the lungs, but in Hill's case plagued his skin. Hill had to travel to Stockholm for treatment, where he remained hospitalized for six months. The operations he underwent left him permanently scarred.

Travels to New World

In 1902 Hill's mother died. Hill and his five siblings, all adults by that time, sold the family house and divided the money. They then went their separate ways. Hill and one of his brothers set off for America—a nation heralded as the land where it was possible to make more in a single day than a person could make in an entire year in Sweden.

The Hill brothers landed in New York in October 1902 and settled in a Swedish section of the city. Hill worked when he could find it and played his violin in his spare time. In 1903 Hill grew tired of New York and headed west to Chicago, Illinois.

Discovers wretched working conditions

Hill found work in a factory in Chicago earning $1.50 to $2.00 for each twelve-hour day. He attempted to improve conditions in the factory by bringing the workers together into a union. Hill was fired for that action and in 1904 left Chicago.

The details of Hill's existence over the next few years

are sketchy, but it is believed that he was constantly on the move. He became part of the tide of migrant workers—most of them immigrants or African Americans—who traveled the country in search of work. It is believed that Hill found employment as a lumberjack in the Pacific Northwest in winter, as a miner in the mountain states in summer, and as a farm laborer in the Midwestern states in fall. Between jobs he rode the rails (stowed away on freight trains) like other "hobos," as they were called, and ate at soup kitchens.

The hobos were unwelcome in most towns. They were greeted by law enforcement officials or vigilantes (citizens who assume police powers without authority) and driven out by force. The hobos were treated just as poorly by employers, who were quick to take advantage of the fact that there were always more prospective workers than there were positions. Certain that they could find people desperate enough to take any job, employers paid the lowest possible wage and made their employees work long hours, six or seven days a week.

Organizes for the IWW

Hill was in San Francisco, California, during the great earthquake of 1906, as evidenced by an article he dispatched to his hometown newspaper about the tragedy. From that point on, Hill made his home in the West. He took on the name "Joe Hill," sometimes calling himself "Joseph Hillstrom." The name change was made either to sound more "American" and less like a foreigner (and thus lessen the anti-immigrant discrimination he would otherwise suffer), or because his reputation as an agitator (one who works for change) was making it difficult for him to find employment.

In 1910 Hill joined an up-and-coming, radical labor union, the IWW. The IWW differed from other unions because it sought to include workers of all races, both genders, all skill levels, and all professions, from all around the world. The other labor unions typically excluded nonwhites and women and formed separate organizations for workers in different trades and different skill levels. The IWW, which characterized capitalism as "wage-slavery," had as its ultimate goal a workers' overthrow of the capitalist system worldwide. In the early 1900s, when unemployment in the United States reached 35 percent, the IWW's message found a receptive audience.

"Rebel Girl" Elizabeth Gurley Flynn

One of Hill's friends and comrades in the movement was activist Elizabeth Gurley Flynn (1890–1964). Flynn was from an Irish working-class family; her parents were both socialists (people who believed the means of production should not be controlled by owners, but by the community as a whole), and her mother was a suffragist (a supporter of women's right to vote [that right was granted in 1920]).

Flynn made her first speech, on women's rights and socialism, before she turned sixteen and by seventeen had become an organizer for the IWW. Throughout her life Flynn organized many strikes, set up defense committees for workers facing police violence and immigrant activists facing deportation, and cofounded the American Civil Liberties Union (ACLU). She was also the first woman to head the American national committee of the Communist Party. When Hill was facing his death sentence, Flynn raised funds for his defense.

In 1915, while he was in prison, Hill wrote *The Rebel Girl* as a tribute to Flynn.

The Rebel Girl

There are women of many descriptions
In this queer world, as every one knows,
Some are living in beautiful mansions,
And are wearing the finest of clothes.
There are blue-blooded queens and princesses,
Who have charms made of diamonds
*   and pearl;*

Hill went to work as an organizer for the IWW. With his easy manner, good sense of humor, and musical talents, he became well-known and well-liked. For four years Hill traveled up and down the West Coast, encouraging workers to go on strike and teaching labor protest songs that he had written. Many of his songs (two of the most popular were "The Preacher and the Slave" and "Rebel Girl") spread by word of mouth and were sung by laborers throughout the country. Hill also submitted articles and comic strips to the IWW newspaper.

Trouble in Utah

In January 1914 Hill was arrested for the murder of a grocery store owner and his son in Salt Lake City, Utah. While a number of things pointed to Hill as the killer, all evidence

Elizabeth Flynn. *Reproduced by permission of Underwood & Underwood/Corbis Corporation.*

But the only and Thoroughbred Lady
Is the Rebel Girl.

Chorus:
That's the Rebel Girl. That's the Rebel Girl.
To the working class she's a precious pearl.
She brings courage, pride and joy
To the Fighting Rebel Boy.
We've had girls before
But we need some more
In the Industrial Workers of the World,
For it's great to fight for freedom
With a Rebel Girl.

Yes, her hands may be harden'd from labor
And her dress may not be very fine;
But a heart in her bosom is beating
That is true to her class and her kind.
And the grafters in terror are trembling
When her spite and defiance she'll hurl.
For the only and Thoroughbred Lady
Is the Rebel Girl.

was circumstantial. According to the survivor of the attack in grocery store, one of the three assailants had been shot. Hill, it turns out, was treated for a gunshot wound that night. Hill's blood, however, was not found at the scene, and the murder weapon was never recovered. Hill claimed he had been shot by a man in a fight over a woman. Hill refused to reveal the woman's name in order to protect her honor—thus depriving himself of an alibi.

Hill was convicted of murder in a speedy trial and sentenced to death. Many people believed that Hill had been framed as punishment for leading a successful strike at United Construction Company in Bingham, Utah, the previous year. Hill's sentence was opposed by President Woodrow Wilson (1856–1924; president 1913–21), the Swedish ambassador to the United States, labor leader Samuel Gompers, and thou-

Joe Hill's Farewell Letter

Shortly before his execution, Joe Hill wrote a farewell letter to his friends:

Dear friends and fellow workers:

'John Law' [generic term for law enforcement authority] has given me his last and final order to get off the earth and stay off. He has told me that lots of times before, but this time it seems as if he is meaning business.

I have said time and again that I was going to get a new trial or die trying. I have told it to my friends. It has been printed in the newspapers, and I don't see why I should 'eat my own crow' just because I happen to be up against a firing squad. I have stated my position plainly to everybody, and I won't budge an inch, because I know I am right. Tomorrow I expect to take a trip to the planet Mars and if so, will immediately commence to organize the Mars canal workers into the IWW, and we will sing the good old songs so loud that the learned star gazers on earth will once and for all get positive proofs that the planet Mars really is inhabited. In the mean time I hope you'll keep the ball a-rolling here. You are on the right track, and you are bound to get there. I have nothing to say about myself, only that I have always tried to do what little I could to make this earth a little better for the great producing class, and I can pass off into the great unknown with the pleasure of knowing that I have never in my life doublecrossed man, woman, or child.

With a last fond farewell to all true rebels and a hearty thanks for the noble support you have given me in this unequal fight, I remain,

Yours for International Solidarity,
Joe Hill

sands of IWW members around the world. The governor of Utah, however, refused to reopen the case.

Death by firing squad

Hill was executed by firing squad on November 19, 1915. In accordance with his stated wish ("I don't want to be found dead in Utah"), Hill's body was transported to IWW headquarters in Chicago. Tens of thousands of mourners came to pay their final respects.

Hill was cremated and his ashes distributed to IWW locals around the world. On May 1, 1916 (the workers' holiday called May Day), Hill's ashes were scattered to the wind in every state of the United States, except Utah. His legendary status continued to grow after his death.

Sources

Books

Button, John. *The Radicalism Handbook*. London, England: Cassell, 1995.

Dubofsky, Melvyn. "Hill, Joe." *American National Biography*. Vol. 10. Edited by John A. Garraty and Mark C. Carnes. New York: Oxford University Press, 1999.

Kornbluh, Joyce L., ed. *Rebel Voices: An IWW Anthology*. Chicago: Charles H. Kerr Publishing Company, 1988.

Loustrup, Soren. *Shattered Dreams: Joe Hill*. Mankato, MN: Creative Education, 1982.

Stegner, Wallace. *Joe Hill: A Biographical Novel*. Lincoln: University of Nebraska Press, 1950.

Articles

Binder, David. "A Little Piece of Joe Hill." *New York Times*. November 17, 1988: B18.

Abbie Hoffman

Born November 30, 1936
Worcester, Massachusetts
Died April 12, 1989
New Hope, Pennsylvania

Social activist and author

> We ended the idea that you can send a million soldiers ten thousand miles away to fight in a war that people do not support. . . . We were young, we were reckless, arrogant, silly, headstrong—and we were right.
>
> *Abbie Hoffman in a speech*
> *at Vanderbilt University,*
> *April 1989*

Abbie Hoffman.
Reproduced by permission of
Corbis Corporation (Bellevue).

A bbie Hoffman was one of the most outspoken and outrageous radicals in American history. He combined biting humor with traditional organizing techniques to protest racism, war, capitalism, greed, polluting industries, and moral puritanism. In an effort to ridicule and devalue institutions he felt were evil, Hoffman threw money on the floor of the New York Stock Exchange, tried to "levitate" the Pentagon, and turned a Chicago, Illinois, courtroom into a circus. Hoffman also made headlines as environmentalist "Barry Freed" (an alias Hoffman used) while on the run from cocaine charges in the 1970s.

A troublemaker from the start

Abbie (full name Abbott) Hoffman was born on November 30, 1936, in Worcester, Massachusetts, the oldest of three children of John Hoffman and Florence Schanberg. John Hoffman was a pharmacist who, in the mid-1940s, founded a medical supply company. The rebellious Abbie and his disciplinarian father were constantly at odds. Abbie described his mother, on the other hand, as loving, accepting, and humorous. In his autobiography, *Soon to be a Major Motion Picture*,

Abbie credited his mother with shooing away the police when he switched license plates on cars in the neighborhood.

Hoffman was an excellent student, but resistant to authority. He was expelled from Classical High School following a fight with an English teacher who had ripped up his paper on atheism and called him a "little communist." Hoffman transferred to the private Worcester Academy where he earned straight A's but consistently received failing grades for conduct.

Becomes politicized in college

After high school Hoffman continued his studies at Brandeis University in Waltham, Massachusetts. There he studied under the Marxist (an adherent of the teachings of German revolutionary socialist thinker **Karl Marx**, (1818–1883; see entry) philosopher Herbert Marcuse (1898–1979). The German-born Marcuse, who had fled to the United States when the Nazis (the authoritarian party headed by Adolf Hitler) rose to power in Germany, was noted for his critique of modern society—especially what he viewed as the substitution of material goods for fundamental freedoms.

Another of Hoffman's mentors was psychology professor Abraham Maslow (1908–1970), whose approach to psychology emphasized love and creativity as driving human needs. Maslow taught Hoffman that rebellion was a healthy way of recognizing one's human potential.

After graduating from Brandeis with a bachelor of arts degree in psychology in 1959, Hoffman went to graduate school at the University of California-Berkeley. While working toward a master's degree in psychology, Hoffman was introduced to the political issues that touched off the turbulent 1960s—civil rights, free speech, and opposition to U.S. military involvement in Vietnam.

Participates in civil rights movement

In 1960 Hoffman married his girlfriend Sheila, who was expecting their child. (The marriage was stormy and ended in divorce six years later; they had two children.) The couple settled in Worcester, where Hoffman worked as a psychologist at Worcester State Hospital.

Hoffman became involved in the growing civil rights movement, volunteering for the **National Association for the Advancement of Colored People** (NAACP; see entry), the Congress on Racial Equality (CORE), and the **Student Nonviolent Coordinating Committee** (SNCC; see entry). From 1963 to 1965 Hoffman worked as a traveling salesman selling medical supplies. That job provided him with a car and enabled him to travel to civil rights demonstrations.

In 1964 Hoffman participated in the Freedom Summer—the intensive summer-long civil rights campaign in Mississippi, organized by the SNCC. The effort involved some one thousand northerners (most of them white college students) who went south as volunteers to conduct voter registration campaigns and educational and social programs. Hoffman returned to the South in 1965 as a SNCC civil rights worker. The following year he moved to New York City and founded Liberty House, a store that sold crafts made by poor people in Mississippi's cooperatives.

Joins opposition to Vietnam War

In 1967 Hoffman joined the growing opposition movement to the Vietnam War (1954–75). At the time he was living in New York City's East Village, a haven for hippies. Hippies were young people who shunned materialism and strict moral codes and embraced communal living, the use of recreational drugs, and sexual liberation.

Hoffman mingled with the hippies, attempting to direct their creative energy into a movement for social change. "Personally, I always held my flower in a clenched fist," wrote Hoffman in *Soon to be a Major Motion Picture*. "A semi-structure freak among the love children, I was determined to bring the hippie movement into a broader protest."

Embarrasses Wall Street in money-throwing incident

In April 1967 Hoffman and a group of hippy-activists took on the bastion of American capitalism: Wall Street. In one of his most famous stunts, Hoffman and his friends threw handfuls of dollar-bills from the visitors gallery onto the floor of the New York Stock Exchange during a busy trading day. The stockbrokers pushed each other aside in a mad scramble for the money. The event was captured in photographs and made the front pages of newspapers around the world.

The Wall Street episode, like the later Pentagon incident (see below), according to Morris Dickstein of the *New York Times Book Review,* "had a clear political goal: to remove the aura of legitimacy from what [Hoffman] saw as unjust and oppressive authority."

Attempts to exorcize the Pentagon

On October 21, 1967, Hoffman convinced 75,000 people, gathered in Washington, D.C., to protest the Vietnam War, to participate in one of the most bizarre demonstrations in history. Hoffman said he had been informed that five-sided symbols were evil and, accordingly, was going to conduct a mass "exorcism of demons" at the Pentagon, a five-sided building. The exorcism involved encircling the military headquarters and attempting, through mental force, to levitate (lift) the building three hundred feet off the ground. Although the action failed to actually raise the Pentagon, it did manage to lift the spirits and kindle the imaginations of the weary protesters.

In 1967 Hoffman entered into his second marriage, with Anita Kushner. The couple had one child, a son named America, and divorced in 1980. Hoffman never remarried after that, but lived for several years with a companion named Johanna Lawrenson.

Co-founds Youth International Party (Yippies)

In 1968 Hoffman and fellow-activist Jerry Rubin founded the Youth International Party, better known as the Yippies. (Hoffman jokingly stated that Yippies was an acronym for "Yiddish Hippies.") The Yippies were a loosely organized group with no leaders, no membership rolls, and no platform. Instead of meetings they held gatherings called Festivals of Life that featured rock music, guerrilla theater (plays dealing with controversial social and political issues), and poetry readings.

The Yippies engaged in a struggle for personal and political freedom using humor and theatrics. They denounced

The Chicago Conspiracy Trial

Hoffman was identified as a ringleader of the protests at the 1968 Democratic National Convention in Chicago, along with seven others, and charged with conspiracy to incite a riot. Although Hoffman had been arrested more than thirty times previously, the Chicago charges were the most serious he had faced to date. Hoffman's co-defendants included Jerry Rubin, Tom Hayden of **Students for a Democratic Society** (see entry), Dave Dellinger and Rennie Davis from the National Mobilization to End the War in Vietnam, Bobby Seale of the **Black Panther Party** (see entry), and two other activists named Lee Weiner and John Froines. Seale, who refused to be quiet in the courtroom, was bound and gagged by the judge. A mistrial was declared in his case and he was removed from the defendants list.

The Chicago Seven, as the group was known after the dismissal of Seale, claimed they had only come to Chicago to stage a peaceful protest. Hoffman employed the same antics in the courtroom as he had in the streets, turning the trial into one of the most celebrated examples of political theatrics in U.S. history.

On the first day of the twenty-week trial Hoffman jokingly announced that he was the illegitimate son of the Vietnam War and the American political and economic system. The Yippies attracted to their ranks such notables as beat-generation poet Allen Ginsberg (1926–1997) and folk singer Phil Ochs (1940–1976).

Yippies protest at 1968 Democratic National Convention

Nineteen-sixty-eight was a tumultuous year in the United States. Both civil rights leader **Martin Luther King, Jr.,** (1929–1968; see entry) and reformist politician Robert F. Kennedy (1925–1968) were assassinated. And while the Vietnam War was being fought on the other side of the world, the struggle for peace was raging in the streets of America. Robert F. Kennedy, who had been the top Democratic contender for the presidential nomination until his death, had called for an

judge, whose name happened to be Julius Hoffman, although the two were not related. Hoffman further eroded the judge's composure when he wore black judicial robes to court. Another day Hoffman entered the courtroom doing a series of somersaults. The defendants regularly refused to stand when the judge entered the courtroom.

The defendants' antics infuriated the judge, who made no effort to be impartial on the bench. "[Judge Hoffman] reminded me [more] of the Queen in Alice in Wonderland," wrote defense attorney William Kunstler (1919–1995), "with her cries, 'Off with their heads,' than a dignified judicial figure." Evidence later surfaced that the judge had cooperated with the Federal Bureau of Investigation (FBI) in illegally taping private meetings between the defendants and their lawyers during the trial.

All the defendants were acquitted of conspiracy charges. Hoffman, Rubin, Dellinger, Davis, and Hayden were convicted of the lesser charge of "crossing state lines with intent to riot" and sentenced to five years in prison. Their convictions were later overturned on appeal. Kunstler was found guilty of twenty-four counts of contempt of court, all but two of which were thrown out on appeal.

end to the Vietnam War. Hubert Humphrey, the second-runner who ultimately received the Democratic nomination, was less committed to peace.

The Democratic National Convention, held in Chicago, Illinois, in August 1968, did not just attract politicians; it attracted throngs of antiwar and antiracism protesters—among them some 2,500 Yippies. Hoffman and other Yippies danced, sang, and smoked marijuana. They promoted a live pig, named Pigasus, as their presidential candidate.

Police were ordered by Chicago mayor Richard Daley (1902–1976; mayor 1955–76) to break up the protest. Television coverage of the convention was moved outside when police began to beat protesters with billy clubs and used tear gas. Members of the media also experienced beatings at the hands of the police.

Abbie Hoffman (center) surrounded by fellow activists at a 1970 press conference.
Reproduced by permission of Corbis-Bettmann.

Enjoys the post-trial limelight

Hoffman emerged from the Chicago conspiracy trial an international celebrity. He went on the lecture circuit throughout the United States and Europe and continued writing. Hoffman's fame boosted sales of his 1968 *Revolution for the Hell of It,* a treatise that rallied young people to transform society. The book was described by Jack Newfield in the *New York Times Book Review* as "a serious manifesto for the growing counter-culture of mind drugs, rock bands, sexual freedom, mixed media, communes, Free Stores, astrology, colorful costumes, and casual nudity."

In 1971 Hoffman published *Steal This Book,* a manual for undermining the capitalist system through theft. "Capitalism is license to steal," wrote Hoffman in the book. "The government simply regulates who steals and how much. I always wanted to put together an outlaw handbook that would help raise consciousness on these points while doing something about evening the score." The book—which many bookstores refused to carry on the grounds that it promoted illegal activity—provided instructions for shoplifting, creating false identification, and making free phone calls from pay phones.

Arrested on cocaine charges; goes underground

On August 28, 1973, Hoffman was arrested on charges of possessing three pounds of cocaine. He had been caught in an undercover sting operation, acting as the middleman in which both seller and buyer were cops. Believing he would not get a fair trial, and facing a minimum fifteen-year prison sentence, Hoffman jumped bail and went underground.

After undergoing plastic surgery and adopting a new walk, gestures, and manner of speech, Hoffman went on the road. He lived in Mexico, Canada, and a variety of other places, using more than twenty aliases. During that time he granted several interviews to national magazines, served as travel editor for *Crawdaddy* magazine, and published two books and more than thirty articles.

Hoffman spent his last four years as a fugitive in Thousand Islands, in upstate New York. He remade himself as a freelance writer and clean-cut environmentalist named "Barry Freed." Freed organized the successful "Save the River" campaign to prevent the U.S. Army Corps of Engineers from dredging the Hudson River (that action, which would have allowed winter-time navigation, would have wreaked havoc on the ecology of the river). Freed was highly visible during the campaign, appearing on local radio and television programs, testifying before a U.S. Senate subcommittee on the environment, receiving a commendation from the governor of New York for his conservation work, serving on a federal water resources commission, and even attending the inauguration of President Jimmy Carter (1924–; president 1977–81).

Serves time, resumes life as environmentalist

On September 3, 1980, Hoffman granted a television interview to Barbara Walters. The next day, dressed as Groucho Marx, he presented himself to law enforcement authorities in New York City. Hoffman pleaded guilty to the possession charge and received a reduced sentence of two months in jail, followed by ten months in a work-release program. Hoffman's reentrance into society provided tremendous publicity for his just-released autobiography, *Soon to be a Major Motion Picture.*

After completing his sentence Hoffman moved back upstate and resumed life as Freed, the environmentalist. In the early 1980s he organized a successful effort to block the building of a nuclear waste processing plant on the Delaware River.

Throughout the 1980s Hoffman made his living giving lectures at universities throughout the country. He spoke out against apartheid (the South African policy of racial segregation and discrimination against blacks and other people of color; dismantled in the early 1990s) and U.S. involvement in the political affairs of Central America.

Opposes CIA recruitment with Amy Carter

Hoffman's final political campaign took place in 1987, when he joined forces with Amy Carter—daughter of former president Jimmy Carter—in opposing recruitment by the Central Intelligence Agency (CIA) on college campuses. Hoffman and Carter were arrested, with thirteen others, on charges of trespassing and disorderly conduct in November 1987 after disrupting CIA recruitment at the University of Massachusetts.

Hoffman and Carter pleaded "not guilty" to the charges and used their trial to "put the CIA on trial." They described the CIA's lawlessness in inciting military coups in other nations, such as Guatemala, Iran, and Nicaragua, and claimed that by disrupting CIA business they were preventing a greater harm (CIA crimes) from occurring. "I believe that we should not have a CIA that goes around overwhelming governments and assassinating political leaders," stated Hoffman in an interview with the *New York Times,* "working for tight oligarchies around the world to protect the tight oligarchy here at home." The protesters were acquitted of all charges.

Dies of drug overdose

In the mid-1980s Hoffman was busy compiling notes and articles for his forthcoming book on manic-depressive disorder—a disease from which he had suffered for a long time. Before he could complete that work, however, he was overcome with depression and took his own life. Hoffman died of a drug overdose on April 12, 1989.

Approximately one thousand mourners attended Hoffman's memorial service in his hometown of Worcester. Folk singer Pete Seeger (1919–) led the crowd in a musical procession and symbolic peace march. Timothy Leary, Hoffman's friend and proponent of drug use in the 1960s, eulogized Hoffman as an "American legend, right up there in the hall of fame with rebel Huck Finn, rowdy Babe Ruth, and crazy Lenny Bruce. He was a hustler, a base stealer, a wild free spirit and a gambler."

Hoffman—who had been arrested fifty-three times and had been banned by eleven state legislatures from entering their states—never softened his criticism of U.S. political and economic systems. "I believe in the redistribution of wealth and power in the world," Hoffman stated in a 1987 interview with the *New York Times*. "I believe in universal hospital care for everyone. I believe that we should not have a single homeless person in the richest country in the world."

Sources

Books

Hoffman, Abbie. *Square Dancing in the Ice Age.* Boston: South End Press, 1982.

Hoffman, Abbie. *Soon to be a Major Motion Picture.* New York: Putnam, 1980.

Hoffman, Abbie. *Steal This Book.* New York: Private Editions, Inc., 1971.

Hoffman, Abbie. *Steal This Urine Test: Fighting Drug Hysteria in America.* New York: Penguin Books, 1987.

Hoffman, Jack, and Daniel Simon. *Run, Run, Run: The Lives of Abbie Hoffman.* New York: G. P. Putnam's Sons, 1994.

Jezer, Marty. *Abbie Hoffman: American Rebel.* New Brunswick, NJ: Rutgers University Press, 1992.

Sloman, Larry. *Steal This Dream: Abbie Hoffman and the Countercultural Revolution in America.* New York: Doubleday, 1998.

Articles

Bernstein, Fred. "Amy Carter and Abbie Hoffman Win Acquittal, but They Want to Keep the CIA on Trial." *People Weekly*. May 4, 1987: 57+.

Buhle, Paul. "The Best of Abbie Hoffman." Review of *Tikkun*. January-February 1993: 68+.

King, Wayne. "Mourning and Celebrating a Radical." *New York Times*. April 20, 1989: A16.

Krassner, Paul. "Abbie." (Editorial.) *The Nation*. May 8, 1989: 626+.

Leo, John. "A Lesson from the Deep, Dark '60s." *U.S. News and World Report*. May 15, 1989: 61.

McQuiston, John T. "Abbie Hoffman, 60's Icon, Dies; Yippie Movement Founder Was 52." *New York Times*. April 14, 1989: D17.

Patricia Ireland

Born October 19, 1945
Oak Park, Illinois

Women's rights activist
and lawyer

Patricia Ireland went to law school in the 1970s with the aim of defending women, workers, and victims of human rights abuses. Instead she wound up working for one of Miami, Florida's most prestigious corporate firms. She rose through the ranks, breaking the "glass ceiling" that typically keeps women out of the top positions. Frustrated by the seemingly shallow purpose of her work, Ireland volunteered to be Florida NOW's (National Organization of Women) legal counsel and threw herself into the women's movement.

In the late 1970s Ireland fought for passage of the Equal Rights Amendment and in the 1980s participated in the abortion rights movement. She moved to Washington, D.C., in the late 1980s to serve as vice president of national NOW and in 1991 ascended to the group's presidency. At the helm of NOW Ireland adopted an "inside/outside" strategy—one that involves promoting sympathetic candidates for elected office while at the same time keeping public pressure on Congress to advance a women's rights agenda.

"When I look at how far we've come, I am thrilled and inspired. . . . But we must be realistic about how serious the threats to women's progress are. The progress we have made was not inevitable, and it is not irreversible."

Patricia Ireland, in What Women Want.

Patricia Ireland.
Reproduced by permission of AP/Wide World Photos.

269

Childhood in Illinois

Patricia Ireland was born on October 19, 1945, in Oak Park, Illinois. She spent most of her childhood in rural Valparaiso, Indiana, where her family raised bees. Ireland's father, James Ireland, worked as a metallurgical engineer, and her mother, Joan Filipek, was a volunteer counselor before becoming director of the local Planned Parenthood (an organization that provides reproductive health services to women and girls). When Ireland was four years old, her older sister Kathy died in a horseback riding accident. The tragedy had great emotional consequences for Ireland. Nevertheless, she describes her childhood as a happy one.

Ireland did well in high school. She not only made the honor roll, she also won a school beauty contest. At the age of sixteen Ireland graduated from high school and entered DePauw University in Greencastle, Indiana, with the plan to become a teacher.

Education, marriage, and divorce

During her second year in college Ireland married a Ball State student named Don Anderson. The couple then transferred to the University of Tennessee. Within months, however, Ireland recognized that she had made a mistake in marrying so young. She divorced her husband and continued her education, adding German to her major of education. Ireland graduated with a bachelor's degree in 1966.

Ireland remained at the University of Tennessee State and pursued an advanced degree in German. After one year of studying German and teaching the language to undergraduates, she decided she was on the wrong career track and dropped out of school. She returned home to Valparaiso and took a waitressing job.

Life as a flight attendant

In 1967, in an attempt to escape what she viewed as a dead-end future in a small town, Ireland went to work as a flight attendant for Pan American Airlines (Pan Am). She was constantly irritated by the subtle and not-so-subtle sexism, as well as the stringent rules of the job. "We stewardesses had to wear red lipstick and fingernail polish—no other color was acceptable," wrote Ireland in her 1996 autobiography *What Women Want.* "On the ground, our black high heels had to measure at least three inches. . . . Brassieres and slips were required at all times. So was the iron maiden of women's wear: the girdle. . . . If [our grooming supervisor] thought we looked a little heavy, she had the right to stick us on a scale—and suspend us if our weight surpassed company-designated limits."

In one memorable experience, the plane on which Ireland was working had been evacuated due to a bomb threat. The pilot, from the safety of the employees' lounge, ordered Ireland to return to the plane and cook him a steak. Ireland refused. "As blasé as I'd become about bomb threats," she wrote in *What Women Want,* "it suddenly occurred to me that this one might just be the real thing. I had resigned myself to the other hazards of a lowly flight attendant's role: the long hours, low pay, leering passengers, groping copilots. But in that moment I realized that I had no real obligation to lay my own life on the line for our captain's dinner."

In 1968 Ireland married James Humble, an artist whom she had met at the University of Tennessee. The couple moved to Miami, Florida, where Ireland had been stationed as a flight attendant. This marriage worked well. Because of the career aspirations of both, they decided not to have children.

Uncovers sex discrimination in health benefits

The episode that Ireland credits with drawing her into the women's rights movement was her discovery of unequal health benefits for male and female employees of Pan Am. Ireland made that discovery when her husband needed dental work. Ireland was told that her medical insurance did not cover her family members. She learned that while none of the female employees' family members were covered by *their* benefits, all of the male employees' families *were* covered by *their* benefits.

Outraged at the injustice of the policy, Ireland called the local National Organization for Women (NOW) chapter. She was told by a staff attorney that since Pan Am worked on federal contracts, the company was bound to uphold federal government standards of nondiscrimination—including the provision of the same benefits to their employees, regardless of gender. Ireland called the Department of Labor, which forced Pan Am to end the discriminatory practice. Ireland had won her first battle as an activist and her husband received his dental care.

Pursues career in law

Ireland's fight for equal benefits inspired her to pursue a career in law. She had been impressed with the ability of NOW's lawyer to help her win her rights and wanted, herself, to help other victims of discrimination. Ireland enrolled in the law school at Florida State University (she later transferred to the University of Miami). She took courses in labor law, human rights law, and civil rights law, and graduated in 1975.

For all her righteous intentions, Ireland ended up working at a large corporate law firm. She took solace in two facts: that one of her clients was the flight attendants' union at Eastern Airlines and that she was able to help her corporate clients develop affirmative action policies. (Affirmative action is a set of federal government policies that provide increased educational and employment opportunities to racial minorities and women, to overcome past patterns of discrimination.) At the same time, Ireland began a twelve-year stint as the volunteer legal counsel to Dade County NOW. In 1977 Ireland led her NOW chapter in a campaign to defeat the antigay-rights referendum spearheaded by entertainer Anita Bryant.

In 1978 Ireland took a position at an even bigger law firm called Arky, Fried, Stearns, Watson, and Greer. (In her autobiography Ireland affectionately refers to the firm as "Big, Big, and Pig.") "I couldn't escape the fact that most of the time my work involved two wealthy guys fighting for each other's money," Ireland reminisced in *What Women Want.* "And aside from my professional pride, I had to ask myself, 'Who cares if my rich guy wins?'"

Ireland finally quit her job at the law firm when her NOW chapter began picketing a company that Ireland's firm represented. NOW charged the company with trampling on the rights of migrant farm laborers in southern Florida.

Supports the ERA, abortion rights, and lesbian/gay rights

In the early 1970s, while a law student, Ireland had become involved in the campaign to pass the Equal Rights

The Proposed Equal Rights Amendment

At the beginning of the twenty-first century, the rights of women still are not explicitly defined in the United States Constitution. While there are presently numerous laws protecting the rights of women, there is no one piece of sweeping legislation that grants equality to women in all aspects of life. The Equal Rights Amendment (ERA), the proposed constitutional amendment guaranteeing women's rights, was defeated in 1972.

The first time an Equal Rights Amendment was brought before Congress was in 1916. The amendment was drafted and proposed by the suffragist National Women's Party, under the leadership of **Alice Paul** (1885–1977; see entry). For six decades after the defeat of the ERA, Paul continued to work for its passage. Paul, along with many other women's rights activists, managed to bring a weaker version of the original ERA before Congress in 1972. Congress passed the bill and sent it along to the states for ratification (three-fourths of all states must ratify constitutional amendments). While two-thirds of the states ratified the amendment, campaigns by conservative organizations prevented its ratification in the other states.

The Equal Rights Amendment, as it was proposed in 1972, read:

Section 1. Equality of rights under the law shall not be denied by the United States or any state on account of sex.

Section 2. The Congress shall have the power to enforce, by appropriate legislation, the provisions of this article.

Section 3. This amendment shall take effect two years after the date of ratification.

Amendment (ERA; see box). The ERA—which was not ratified by the requisite three-quarters of states and therefore never took effect—would have granted equality to women in all respects of public life.

In the 1980s Ireland shifted her focus to abortion-rights work. Abortion—the termination of an unwanted pregnancy by removing the fetus from the uterus, usually within the first twelve weeks of pregnancy—was made legal in 1973 in the landmark *Roe v. Wade* class action ruling. The battle over abortion rights began immediately after the *Roe* decision. In the mid-1980s antiabortion demonstrators began holding frequent demonstrations in front of clinics where abortions

NOW rally: Stop Violence Against Women.
Reproduced by permission of the Gamma Liaison Network.

are performed. Ireland joined other prochoice activists (the term describing individuals who support abortion rights) in defending clinics and health care personnel from vandalism and violence at the hands of antiabortion protesters.

Ireland, as a NOW leader, also worked hard to protect the rights of lesbians and gay men. From 1983 to 1985 Ireland chaired the Florida NOW task force on lesbian rights. "Until the charge of 'lesbian' carries no sting," stated Ireland in a 1991 interview, "it is a very powerful weapon to keep any woman from standing up and being independent."

Moves to Washington for NOW position

In 1985 Ireland was selected by Eleanor Smeal to be manager of her campaign for the presidency of national NOW. Smeal won the election. Two years later Ireland was asked by another NOW presidential hopeful, Molly Yard, to run as her vice-presidential candidate. Ireland accepted. The pair won the election, and Ireland moved to Washington, D.C., to take her first paid position with NOW.

Yard and Ireland won reelection in 1989. Two years later Ireland took the place of the aging and ailing Yard as NOW president. Ireland was reelected to the presidency of the 250,000-member organization for four-year terms in 1993 and 1997.

Tenure as president of NOW

As president of NOW, Ireland plans strategy, holds press conferences, organizes conferences, leads marches, meets with lawmakers, travels around the country giving lectures, campaigns on behalf of pro-women's-rights political candidates, and supervises a staff of thirty-five workers. In 1999, after many years during which NOW operated at a deficit, Ireland got the group's finances back on track.

As NOW president Ireland has highlighted the needs of poor women, women suffering from domestic violence, and gays and lesbians. In 1996 Ireland was arrested in front of the White House while protesting President Bill Clinton's proposed welfare reform legislation. The legislation, which became law that fall, dismantled the federal government's welfare program, Aid to Families with Dependent Children, and transferred responsibility for welfare programs to the states.

After her 1997 reelection Ireland announced a campaign to elect two thousand feminist women to office by the year 2000. "We must fight to maintain the gains we have made over the past thirty years," Ireland stated in her acceptance speech, "but we cannot be satisfied with the status quo."

Ireland's presidential tenure has been marked by a willingness to work both inside and outside of "the system." She believes that it is just as valuable to get sympathetic candidates elected to office, and to hold meetings with elected officials, as it is to hold rallies or marches. "I don't think that we can make change only from the outside," Ireland stated in a 1999 interview with *The Progressive*. "I think we have to get some people inside. And getting people inside means that they're going to have to be willing to fight as hard as they can, with us perhaps strengthening their hand by being as rowdy and obnoxious as we can."

Downplays controversy over private life

Since becoming president of NOW, Ireland's personal life has come under scrutiny. She has admitted to having a long-term relationship with a woman, even while married to a man. Ireland downplays the relevance of her personal life in her position as the leader of NOW. "I am absolutely determined to resist our culture's obsession with evaluating women on the basis of our sexuality," she wrote in *What Women Want.*

Sources

Books

Ireland, Patricia. *What Women Want.* New York: Dutton, 1996.

"Ireland, Patricia." *Current Biography Yearbook.* Edited by Judith Graham. New York: H. W. Wilson Company, 1992.

"Patricia Ireland." *Encyclopedia of World Biography.* 2nd ed. Detroit: Gale Research, 1998.

Articles

Blow, Richard. "What Patricia Wants: NOW's President Celebrates the Organization's 30th Anniversary." *Mother Jones.* September-October 1996: 70+.

Conniff, Ruth. "Patricia Ireland." *The Progressive.* August 1999: 35+.

Cool, Lisa Collier. "The New Leadership." *Cosmopolitan.* May 1994: 206+.

"Ireland Reelected President of NOW." *Los Angeles Times.* July 6, 1997: A16.

Kristol, Elizabeth. Review of *What Women Want. Commentary.* September 1996: 83+.

Schneider, Karen S., and Elizabeth Velez. "Too Nice to Be One of 'Those Women'? NOW's New Chief Patricia Ireland." *People Weekly.* January 13, 1992: 93+.

Jesse Jackson

Born October 8, 1941
Greenville, South Carolina

Civil rights leader, politician, and minister

J esse Jackson was thrust into the civil rights spotlight in the 1960s as an aide to **Martin Luther King, Jr.**, (1929–1968; see entry) and director of the Southern Christian Leadership Conference's (SCLC) Operation Breadbasket. In 1971 Jackson formed the Chicago-based organization PUSH (People United to Serve Humanity). He vied for the Democratic presidential nomination in both 1984 and 1988.

Throughout the 1980s and 1990s Jackson continued his civil rights and human rights work: fighting racial discrimination, supporting striking workers, and conducting voter registration drives. He also took on the role of informal international ambassador. In the years spanning 1984 through 1990 Jackson negotiated the liberation of captives being held by the governments of Syria, Cuba, and Iraq. In late 1999 he made national headlines by supporting seven African American youths expelled from a Decatur, Illinois, high school.

Educational achievements

Jackson was born in Greenville, South Carolina, in 1941. He attended Sterling High School in Greenville, where

"When I look out at this convention, I see the face of America: Red, Yellow, Brown, Black and White. We are all precious in God's sight—the real rainbow coalition."

Jesse Jackson, address to the Democratic National Convention, July 19, 1988.

Jesse Jackson.
Reproduced by permission of AP/Wide World Photos.

Jesse Jackson raising his fist to make the Black Power sign after being arrested.
Reproduced by permission of AP/Wide World Photos.

he was president of his class and a star on the school football team. Following his high school graduation in 1959, Jackson was awarded a football scholarship to the University of Illinois.

Jackson left the University of Illinois after one year and transferred to the all-black North Carolina Agricultural and Technical (A&T) College in Greensboro. He attributed his decision to transfer to numerous incidents of racial discrimination he had suffered in Illinois. During Jackson's senior year of college he married Jacqueline Lavinia Brown. The couple eventually had five children: daughters Jacqueline and Santita, and sons Jesse, Jr., Yusef, and Jonathan.

Just months before Jackson arrived in Greensboro, the town had achieved fame as the site of the first lunch-counter sit-ins (a form of protest in which African American students, sometimes joined by white students, requested service at whites-only lunch counters; when the students were denied service, they refused to leave). The Greensboro lunch-counter sit-ins sparked a wave of protests, not only at lunch counters but at all segregated (separated by race) facilities throughout the American South. Jackson soon involved himself in civil rights activities, leading marches and sit-ins at segregated hotels and restaurants.

Jackson completed a bachelor of arts degree in sociology at North Carolina A & T in 1964. He then enrolled in the Chicago Theological Seminary, intending to become a minister. Jackson combined his studies with civil rights activism over the next four years and was ordained a Baptist minister in 1968.

Works with Martin Luther King, Jr.

In 1964 Jackson went to work as the southeastern field director of the Congress on Racial Equality (CORE; an organization that challenged racial segregation). Two years later Jackson was hired by **Martin Luther King, Jr.**, (see entry) to direct the Chicago, Illinois, branch of Operation Breadbasket—an economic development project of the Southern Christian Leadership Conference (SCLC; a civil rights organization led by African American ministers, of which King was president). The goal of Operation Breadbasket was to increase the number of African American workers at white-owned companies, as well as to support African American-owned businesses. Using the boycott as his weapon, Jackson forced many employers (most notably the chain of A & P supermarkets) to hire large numbers of African American workers.

Jackson was so successful that in 1967 he was appointed national director of Operation Breadbasket. In that capacity Jackson organized the first Black Expo, a convention at which African American business owners shared their secrets of success and African American-owned companies displayed their wares.

Jackson also served as an aide to King, frequently traveling with the legendary civil rights leader to sites of civil rights campaigns. Jackson was standing next to King on the balcony of the Lorraine Motel in Memphis, Tennessee, on April 4, 1968, when King was killed by a sniper's bullet. After King's death Jackson had hoped to become the next SCLC president. That honor, however, went to another King aide—Ralph Abernathy (1926–1990).

Forms PUSH

Jackson returned to Illinois after King's death and continued organizing civil rights demonstrations. In 1971 he resigned from the SCLC and founded his own organization, People United to Serve Humanity—better known as PUSH. The purpose of PUSH was to increase the political and economic clout of African Americans, as well as to monitor the affirmative action programs in large corporations. (Affirmative action is a set of federal government policies that provide increased educational and employment opportunities to racial minorities and women to overcome past patterns of discrimination.) Under Jackson's directorship, PUSH won agreements with Burger King, Kentucky Fried Chicken, General Foods, Schlitz Breweries, and other corporations to employ more African American workers, purchase goods and services from African American-owned businesses, and invest in African American banking institutions.

In 1975 Jackson widened PUSH's mission by launching PUSH-Excel, a program that encouraged educational achievement among African American youth. Jackson secured a million-dollar grant from the federal government and went on a tour of inner-city schools. He urged students to sign cards pledging to spend two hours every night on their schoolwork. By 1986 Jackson had set up PUSH chapters in fourteen metropolitan areas, in places as diverse as New York; Los Angeles, California; Memphis, Tennessee; and Columbus, Ohio.

In 1979 Jackson took his fight for racial equality abroad to South Africa. There he led protests against the system of racial segregation called apartheid (apartheid was dismantled in the early 1990s). Jackson's next international mission took him to the Middle East, where he attempted to improve relations between Israelis and the people of occupied Palestine.

Activism in the 1990s

Jackson moved to Washington, D.C., following the 1988 elections. In 1990 he was elected to represent the district in the U.S. Senate—a nonvoting, observer position. Jackson

Jackson's Bids for President

Jackson vied for the Democratic presidential nomination in both 1984 and 1988, becoming the only African American man to have sought the nation's highest office. In both campaigns Jackson attempted to bring together voters of all races in what he called a Rainbow Coalition. In 1984 numerous whites joined with Latinos, Native Americans, and 80 percent of African American voters in securing victories for Jackson in the primaries of South Carolina, Louisiana, and Washington, D.C. At the Democratic National Convention, Jackson received the third-largest number of delegate votes.

In his 1988 campaign Jackson stressed his commitment to creating economic opportunities for all U.S. citizens. He placed first in the primary elections of fourteen states and second in the primaries of thirty-six others. Jackson was backed by 12 percent of white voters in 1988 (three times as many whites backed him that year than in his previous bid). At the national convention Jackson came in second only to Massachusetts Governor Michael Dukakis.

used his presence in the Senate to promote the issue of statehood for the District of Columbia. Also in 1990, just prior to the start of the Gulf War (1991), Jackson traveled to Iraq and negotiated the release of five hundred hostages that had been taken by Iraq during its invasion of neighboring Kuwait. In October 1997 President Bill Clinton appointed Jackson to be his special envoy for the promotion of democracy in Africa.

Throughout the 1990s Jackson continued his advocacy on behalf of African Americans, working people, and other aggrieved groups. In 1991 he spoke out about workplace safety following a fire in a poultry-processing plant in North Carolina that claimed the lives of twenty-five workers and lobbied for treatment for veterans suffering from Gulf War syndrome (the term used to describe a variety of ailments afflicting veterans of the Gulf War). In 1996 Jackson picketed the White House over President Clinton's endorsement of welfare reform—legislation that dismantled the federal government's welfare program, Aid to Families with Dependent Children, and transferred responsibility for welfare programs to the states. The following year Jackson defended affirmative action (the set of federal government policies, primarily in education and employment, that give preferential treatment to racial minorities and women) as the regents of the University of California prepared to dismantle the program.

Rescues American hostages in Yugoslavia

In May 1999 Jackson won a diplomatic coup when he convinced Serbian President Slobodan Milosevic to release three U.S. servicemen being held hostage. The U.S. soldiers— Andrew Ramirez, Christopher J. Stone, and Steven Gonzales— had been captured by Serb forces on March 31 while patrolling the border between Macedonia and Yugoslavia as part of a North Atlantic Treaty Organization (NATO) operation to drive the Serbian army out of the province of Kosovo.

Although Jackson's mission was not endorsed by the U.S. government, the Senate chose to honor him upon his return from Yugoslavia. By a 92-0 vote the Senate commended him for his successful intervention on behalf of the imprisoned servicemen.

Defends expelled students in Decatur, Illinois

In early November 1999 Jackson traveled to Decatur, Illinois, to support seven African American teens who had been expelled from the city's Eisenhower High School. The Decatur school board had voted the month before to bar the youths from the high school for two years, with the option of applying for readmission after one year, for fighting at a football game in September (they later reduced the expulsions to one year). The strict punishment was doled out under the district's "zero tolerance" policy on violence (many districts throughout the United States adopted strict disciplinary rules in the wake of school shootings in Colorado, Arkansas, and other states). Jackson argued that the "zero tolerance" policy was unduly severe and that it disproportionately affected minorities.

In the first two weeks of November, Jackson led thousands of people on two protest marches through Decatur. The marchers chanted: "Save the dream, save the children, reclaim the children," and "Leave no child behind, keep hope alive."

A group of white supremacists from nearby Peoria, Illinois, held a counterdemonstration during one march. On November 16 Jackson upped the stakes by leading a group of ministers and other protesters to Eisenhower High, where they crossed onto school property in defiance of a court order and were arrested. Jackson vowed to continue the pressure until the expelled youths were back in school.

Sources

Books
"Jesse Jackson." *African American Biography,* Vol. 2. Detroit: U•X•L, 1994, pp. 378–82.

Williams, Nicole L. Baily. "Jesse Jackson." *Notable Black American Men.* Edited by Jessie Carney Smith. Farmington Hills, MI: The Gale Group, 1999, pp. 598–602.

Articles
"Jackson and 2,000 Protest Expulsions." *The New York Times.* November 15, 1999: A19.

"Jackson Marches on High School, Is Arrested." *Los Angeles Times.* November 17, 1999: A13.

Johnson, Dirk. "Jackson Arrested in Protest over Expulsions of Students." *The New York Times.* November 17, 1999: A16.

Lombardi, Frank, and William Goldschlag. "Jackson, Cuomo Vent Liberal Opposition to Clinton's Signing of Welfare Bill, but Embrace His Candidacy." *New York Daily News.* (Knight Ridder/Tribune News Service.) August 27, 1996.

Miller, Sabrina L. "PUSH, Rainbow Coalition Still at Heart of Jackson's Work." *The Miami Herald.* (Knight Ridder/Tribune News Service.) May 16, 1999.

"Rev. Jesse Jackson Announces that He Will Not Run for President in 2000." *Jet.* April 12, 1999: 12.

Seipel, Tracy, and Ariana E. Cha. "Protesters March across Golden Gate Bridge to Denounce Proposition 209." *San Jose Mercury News.* (Knight Ridder/Tribune News Service.) August 28, 1997.

Slater, Eric. "One Brawl, Among Many, Catches National Eye." *Los Angeles Times.* November 12, 1999: A16.

Slater, Eric. "Student Expulsions Divide a Town Known for Divides." *Los Angeles Times.* November 21, 1999: A1.

"U.S. Senate Praises Rev. Jackson for Winning Release of POWs." *Jet.* May 24, 1999: 6.

Wei Jingsheng

Born May 20, 1950
Beijing, China

Chinese prodemocracy and human-rights activist

> "Which country has acquired democracy, freedom, and human rights without hard struggle and shedding blood and sweat? You could not possibly wait for someone to present you with a democracy."
>
> *Wei Jingsheng in a 1998 interview with* China News Digest

Wei Jingsheng.
Reproduced by permission of AP/Wide World Photos.

Wei Jingsheng was raised to believe in the communist system and to support China's Communist Party leaders. (Communism is a theory of social organization based on the holding of all property in common, overseen by a centralized government.) He studied the teachings of communist thinkers during his youth. As a teenager he joined the Red Guard—the youth wing of the national forces charged with ensuring allegiance to communist principles and to party chairman Mao Tse-tung (1893–1976).

After witnessing poverty in the countryside, however, Wei became disillusioned with government policies. He became an outspoken critic of China's leaders and a forceful advocate for democracy, for which he spent a total of seventeen years in prison. In 1997 Wei was set free and left the country on a plane bound for the United States.

Son of Communist Party officials

Wei Jingsheng was born on May 20, 1959, in Beijing, China. He was the oldest of four children born to Communist

Party officials. Wei's family lived in a compound, together with the families of several high-ranking party officials, in the center of Beijing. Wei's father, Wei Zilin, was a director of a leading construction agency, and Wei's mother, Du Peijun, was a government official. Wei's family was well acquainted with ruler Mao Tse-tung, his wife (a prominent party official) Jiang Qing, and their son.

Wei was brought up to respect the teachings of Mao and to understand the benefits the nation had experienced under communist rule. He was made to read the works of revolutionary communists **Karl Marx** (1818–1883; see entry), Friedrich Engels (1820–1895), Vladimir Lenin (1870–1924), and Josef Stalin (1879–1953), and to memorize one page each day of the writings of Mao. Wei's mother explained to him that the communist system aimed to raise the standard of living of China's poorest citizens. Wei attended prestigious schools, where he and his classmates were groomed for future careers as Communist Party officials.

Participates in Cultural Revolution

In 1966 Wei joined a Red Guard unit, as did millions of young people with ties to the Communist Party. The Red Guards were youth groups organized by Mao Tse-tung to help carry out his Cultural Revolution (a political program aimed at renewing China's allegiance to revolutionary communism and to Chairman Mao himself—see box). Wei, along with the rest of his Red Guard unit, enthusiastically set out to find people who were not sufficiently supportive of the government. That process involved posing tough questions to party officials, schoolteachers, and other influential people. The questioning in many cases escalated to verbal and physical assaults.

Several months after joining the Red Guard, Wei became part of an elite unit comprised of children of high-ranking party officials, called the United Action Committee. That committee went about rooting out disloyal elements in society with an alarming zeal. Wei, for his part, believed that he was part of a necessary and valuable campaign. Before long, however, the army, on orders from Mao (who decided that things had gotten out of hand), disbanded Wei's unit and other units of the Red Guard, and jailed the units' members.

The Cultural Revolution

The Cultural Revolution, which began in 1966 and lasted through the mid-1970s, was initiated by Communist Party chairman Mao Tse-tung (also spelled Mao Zedong, 1893–1976; the first leader of the People's Republic of China following the 1949 communist revolution) as a means of renewing the nation's allegiance to revolutionary communism. Mao sought to replace the officials designated to rule upon his retirement with people more committed to his own way of government. At the same time, Mao saw the opportunity for providing China's young people with a means of demonstrating their revolutionary spirit.

To accomplish his goals, Mao organized youth groups called Red Guards. The role of the Red Guards was to neutralize people and institutions who were not demonstrating loyalty to Mao and the revolution. The Red Guards were ordered to test the resolve of Communist Party officials by criticizing them in public. Events got out of control and many confrontations turned violent. Schoolteachers, party members, and former revolutionary heroes were humiliated, beaten, and even killed. An atmosphere of fear, chaos, and violence reigned. Economic activity in the cities was brought to a standstill.

The Red Guards, dispatched around the nation, splintered into enemy factions. Each faction claimed to be the true representative of Maoist doctrine. Armed battles between factions created widespread disorder. Mao finally dispatched the army to disband the Red Guards and to scatter their members to China's rural provinces. The Cultural Revolution, which came to be recognized as Mao's personal bid to consolidate power, led to widespread disillusionment within the Chinese populace.

Wei was imprisoned for the first few months of 1967. Upon his release, Wei, like others in the Red Guard, was pressured to move to the countryside. (Mao wanted Red Guard members out of urban areas, where most of the violence had occurred).

Changes views during years in countryside

Wei headed for his family's ancestral homeland in central China: Chao County, in rural Anhui Province. There Wei found that the communist policies, which had brought relative prosperity to the cities, had left the rural population behind. He was told by peasants that Mao's programs had actually intensified poverty and hunger in the remote countryside. Wei began to doubt the very principles he had fought so ardently to preserve just months earlier.

Lacking better prospects, Wei enlisted in the army in 1969. There, in the midst of the mostly peasant force, Wei's doubts about China's communist program intensified. His tour of duty took him throughout the countryside, where he discovered that rural poverty was widespread.

Returns to Beijing; solidifies opposition beliefs

Wei was discharged from the army in 1973 and returned to Beijing. He found his career options limited because, during the Cultural Revolution, his parents had fallen out of favor with the Communist Party leadership (his father had actually been sentenced to a term in a labor camp). Wei received vocational training and found a job as an electrician at the Beijing Zoo.

By that time Wei had become deeply critical of the government, which was defined by Mao as a "people's democratic dictatorship." "If you want democracy, folks will get together to discuss diverse opinions," stated Wei in a *China News Daily* article. "If you have dictatorship, nobody can discuss with you. . . . If you still had to listen to [the ruler], then what was the point of democracy?"

Another influence on Wei's thinking in that period was his relationship with a Tibetan woman named Ping Ni. Ping's family had suffered greatly during the Maoist takeover of Tibet in 1950 and the forcible suppression of an uprising against Chinese rule in 1959. Ping's father was languishing in a prison camp and her mother had committed suicide.

Places provocative poster on Democracy Wall

In 1976, with the death of Chairman Mao, came a slight relaxation of social controls and a greater freedom to dissent. Democracy Wall—located just west of Tiananmen Square in the center of Beijing—was established in 1978 as a focal point for political discussion. Students, workers, and other interested individuals would paste posters stating their opinions on this wall. Very few of the posters, however, questioned the ideals of communism and the Chinese style of government (most merely criticized individual leaders).

Wei put up a poster that appealed for democracy. "We want to be masters of our own destiny," Wei wrote. "Democracy, freedom, and happiness for all are our sole objectives. . . ." Wei's poster, to which he signed his name, became very popular. Many young people sought out Wei and together they started a prodemocracy newspaper called *Exploration*. Among the topics they addressed were the human rights abuses heaped on political prisoners by Chinese authorities.

Wei was well aware that his activism could lead to his arrest, yet he remained steadfast in his mission. "Which country has acquired democracy, freedom, and human rights without hard struggle and shedding blood and sweat?" he stated in a 1998 interview with *China News Digest*. "You could not possibly wait for someone to present you with a democracy."

Convicted of counterrevolutionary acts

On March 19, 1979, a law was passed prohibiting the publication of anticommunist writings. In response, Wei published the most outspoken issue of *Exploration* to date. On March 29, Wei was arrested at his home by twenty armed officers. Wei was put in jail, his head was shaved, and he was made to wear a prison uniform. It was in that attire that Wei attended his trial, on October 16, 1979.

Wei was charged with committing counterrevolutionary acts. The prosecutor stated, "The citizen has only the freedom to support [communist] principles, and not the freedom to oppose them." In his own defense, Wei did not deny his actions but claimed that he had done nothing wrong. Wei responded, "Some people have the following view: it is revolutionary to act in accordance with the will of the leaders in power and counterrevolutionary to oppose the will of the people in power. I cannot agree with this debasing of the concept of revolution. Revolution is the struggle between the old and the new. . . . The current historical tide is a democratic one, which opposes feudal, fascist dictatorship."

Wei's guilt was a foregone conclusion in the eyes of the court. He was sentenced to fifteen years in prison.

Difficult years in prison

Wei's first five years in prison were spent in solitary confinement (a very long time to be alone by any standards). He was often beaten by guards. His nutritionally inadequate prison diet led to gum disease and the eventual loss of twelve of his teeth. Wei experienced other health problems too, such as hepatitis and a heart condition.

Wei was transferred to a prison labor camp in the countryside for the second five years of his sentence. Prison officials believed that subjecting Wei to hard work at a high altitude would exacerbate his heart condition and make him die of natural causes. Being outdoors and having contact with other prisoners, however, led to an improvement in Wei's health and spirits. In 1989 Wei was transferred to another prison, called the Nangpu New Life Salt Works, to serve the remainder of his sentence.

A six-month taste of freedom

Wei was released one year before the completion of his sentence, on September 14, 1993. His early release was a public-relations move on the part of the Chinese government, which had put in a bid to host the year 2000 Olympics Games. The government's gesture had been in vain, as China was not selected by the International Olympic Committee.

Wei's freedom, however, was short-lived. Immediately upon his release he had resumed his protest activities. Wei was arrested again on April 1, 1994, just four days after a meeting in which he discussed China's human rights record with a U.S. government official.

Wei remained in custody and his whereabouts were kept secret for a year and a half. He was brought to trial in December 1995 and convicted of trying to overthrow the Chinese government. He was sentenced to fourteen years in prison—a sentence that was protested by human-rights organization **Amnesty International** (see entry) and government officials from the United States, France, Germany, and Great Britain.

Freed and exiled to United States

Wei was released from prison on November 16, 1997—

just two years into his sentence—and put on a plane for the United States. His release had been brokered during talks about human rights and economic issues between U.S. President Bill Clinton and China's President Jiang Zemin. On his arrival in Detroit, Michigan, Wei was taken to a hospital for medical treatment.

Although Wei cherished his newfound freedom, he voiced disappointment that he could not be a free man in his own country. During his time in the United States, Wei has granted several interviews and has worked to publicize the plight of political prisoners in China. In December 1997 Wei accepted a position as a visiting scholar at Columbia University's School of International and Public Affairs in New York. In 1998 he was nominated, for the fifth year in a row, for the Nobel Peace Prize for his work on behalf of human rights in China. Also in 1998 Wei was awarded the European Parliament's Sakharov Prize for Freedom of Thought and the Olaf Palme Award (named for the assassinated prime minister of Sweden).

Sources

Books

Jingsheng, Wei. *The Courage to Stand Alone: Letters from Prison and Other Writings.* Translated by Kristina M. Torgeson. New York: Viking Penguin, 1997.

"Wei Jingsheng." *Current Biography Yearbook.* Edited by Elizabeth A. Schick. New York: H. W. Wilson Company, 1997, pp. 594–97.

"Wei Jingsheng." *Encyclopedia of World Biography.* 2nd ed. 18 vols. Detroit: Gale Research, Inc., 1998.

Articles

"A Chinese Exile Comes Calling." *Maclean's.* February 23, 1998: 29.

Jingsheng, Wei. "What to Do about China." *Newsweek.* December 29, 1997: 50.

Wehrfritz, George. "What Now for Wei?" (Interview.) *Newsweek.* December 1, 1997: 42+.

Wehrfritz, George. "He's Free at Last: Beijing Grudgingly Sends its Most Famous Political Prisoner, Wei Jingsheng, into Exile. But What about the Thousands of Others Left Behind?" *Newsweek.* November 24, 1997: 42+.

Mary Harris "Mother" Jones

Born May 1, 1830
Cork, Ireland
Died November 30, 1930
Silver Springs, Maryland

Labor organizer

As a child of Irish rebels, Mary Harris "Mother" Jones grew up understanding the injustices suffered by the poor at the hands of the powerful. She married a union organizer in 1861 and, after losing her husband and four children to yellow fever in 1867, moved to Chicago, Illinois, and became active in the labor movement. At various times affiliated with the Knights of Labor, the Industrial Workers of the World, and the United Mine Workers, Jones was, above all, an independent, unstoppable, and fiery agitator. A self-described "hellraiser," Jones defied police officers, judges, and corporate bosses in her unwavering support for the rights of mine workers, textile workers, and child laborers.

Born to tenant farmers in Ireland

"Mother" Jones was born Mary Harris on May 1, 1830, in Cork Ireland. (Some historians dispute that birth date, claiming she was really born closer to 1840.) Mary grew up in rural Ireland. Her parents were tenant farmers who worked the land of a wealthy estate owner. They were active in the Irish resistance to British rule. Jones stated in her autobiography, "I was born in revolution."

"Perhaps the crime of child slavery has never been forcibly brought to your notice These little children, raked by cruel toil beneath the iron wheels of greed, are starving in this country which you have declared is in the height of prosperity."

Mary Harris "Mother" Jones, letter to a newspaper

Mary Harris "Mother" Jones.
Courtesy of the Library of Congress.

Jones's father, Robert Harris, was forced to flee Ireland in 1835 after participating in a violent uprising of tenant farmers against the landlord. Harris went to the United States and, after becoming a naturalized American citizen in 1841, sent for his family. The Harrises lived for a short time in New York City. Then they moved to Toronto, Canada, where Robert Harris had secured a job building one of the first Canadian railroads.

Education and early work positions

Jones's parents, who were essentially illiterate, made sure that their children took advantage of Toronto's public schools. Jones excelled in school and became the first in her family to graduate from high school. Intent on becoming a teacher, Jones found herself barred from the profession in Toronto because of discrimination against Catholics (Jones's family was Roman Catholic). Jones then moved to the United States and found a tutoring position in Maine. Two years later she accepted a job teaching at a convent in Monroe, Michigan. Uncomfortable with the strict rules of the religious order, Jones left that position after just one year.

Loses family to yellow fever

Mary next moved to Chicago, Illinois, and tried to earn a living as a dressmaker. After struggling financially through the years 1858 and 1859, she decided to try teaching again. Hearing about a need for teachers in Memphis, Tennessee, Jones packed her bags and headed south.

Jones arrived in Memphis in the summer of 1860 and secured a teaching position for the coming fall. Soon after her arrival, she met George Jones, a worker in an iron foundry and a part-time organizer for the Iron Molders' Union. The couple married and over the next six years Mary gave birth to four children. George obtained a full-time position with the union.

The Jones family was financially stable and happy until the yellow fever outbreak of 1867. While people with the resources to leave the city did so, Memphis's poorer citizens fell victim to the epidemic. Medical personnel would not care for the sick, as they were afraid of catching the disease themselves. Mary Jones watched helplessly as her four children and her husband died of the disease. Alone in the world, she devoted herself to aiding other sick people in the community.

Returns to Chicago

When the epidemic ended, Jones had no reason to remain in Memphis. She headed back to Chicago, determined to try to make a living as a seamstress again. Jones set up a small shop and took in work. She was also hired by some of the city's wealthiest residents to come to their homes and make draperies, clothing, and furniture coverings.

Jones was struck by the sharp contrast between the lives of the wealthy people for whom she worked and the lives of the city's poor majority. "Often while sewing for the lords and barons who live in magnificent houses on the Lake Shore Drive," Jones wrote in her autobiography, "I would look out of the plate glass windows and see the poor, shivering wretches, jobless and hungry, walking along the frozen lake front. The contrast of their condition with that of the tropical comfort of the people for whom I sewed was painful to me."

Jones lost her sewing shop and all her possessions in the great Chicago fire of October 1871. The blaze engulfed one-sixth of the city, including the working-class neighborhood in which Jones lived, leaving thousands of people homeless. Jones was taken in by members of the Iron Molders' Union to which her husband had belonged.

Joins Knights of Labor

One night shortly after the fire, Jones came upon a meeting at the office of a union called the Knights of Labor. She went inside and was inspired by what she heard. The goal of the Knights of Labor, Jones learned, was to bring dignity to the lives of people who toiled in factories and mines.

Jones signed up to be a member on the spot. She quickly became active in the union, speaking before groups of workers and setting up union meetings. Before long Jones had given up her job as a seamstress to work full time as a Knights of Labor organizer. Her first assignment, in 1874, was to work in support of a bitter year-long coal-miners' strike in Pennsylvania. There Jones discovered her gift for inspirational oratory and for lifting the morale of strikers' families. The mine workers came to consider Jones their trusted advisor and bestowed upon her the nickname "Mother."

Takes to the road as an independent labor organizer

As Jones's involvement with the labor movement deepened, she became convinced that workers could only win concessions from management through strikes and other direct action tactics—even if those tactics involved violence. Jones's philosophy put her at odds with the Knights of Labor, which had become increasingly opposed to confrontational strategies.

In the mid-1880s Jones parted ways with the Knights and took to the road as an independent labor organizer. She traveled throughout the country, going from one labor hotspot to the next, urging workers to fight for their rights by forming labor unions.

Develops special bond with coal miners

During her sixty years as a union activist Jones supported hundreds of strikes by workers in the mining, railroad, brewing, and textile industries. She gave impassioned speeches to convince workers that by standing together they could win concessions from even the most oppressive bosses.

Jones's greatest dedication, however, was to coal miners. Her "boys," as she called the coal miners (many, indeed, were mere boys), worked long hours in dangerous conditions for low pay. They were housed in dilapidated, company-owned shacks, the rent for which consumed a sizable portion of their paychecks. Furthermore, the miners had no choice but to purchase their necessities at company stores, at greatly inflated prices. Many miners found themselves chronically indebted to mine owners for purchases made on credit. All attempts by the miners to unionize were met with violence at the hands of the mine owners' hired thugs (called the "coal and iron police").

Hired by United Mine Workers

In 1891 Jones was hired as an organizer by the United Mine Workers (UMW) union. She returned to the coal fields of

Pennsylvania, where in the years since the 1874 strike the UMW had made considerable progress in organizing the miners. Jones rallied miners to become active in the union and to fight for better wages and working conditions. In an effort to avoid contact with the coal and iron police, Jones traveled through the miners' camps in disguise and lodged with different families every night.

By the winter of 1899, the union was strong enough to stage a strike. The workers kept the mines closed throughout the cold months. Jones, at age seventy, organized the miners' wives and children to keep scabs (workers hired by bosses to take the place of striking workers) from entering the mines by standing at mine entrances and brandishing mops, brooms, pots, pans, and rolling pins. Jones found that security thugs were less likely to become violent with women and children than they were with men. The strike succeeded, and working conditions for the miners improved considerably.

Fights for rights of child laborers

In 1903 Jones turned her energies toward the plight of children working in factories and mines. In numerous speeches she explained that, due to conditions of poverty, some two million American children had to forego their education and the pleasures of childhood to work long hours at dangerous occupations. "Perhaps the crime of child slavery has never been forcibly brought to your notice," wrote Jones in a letter to a newspaper. "These little children, raked by cruel toil beneath the iron wheels of greed, are starving in this country which you have declared is in the height of prosperity."

In June 1903, when one hundred thousand Philadelphia, Pennsylvania, textile workers—one-sixth of them children under sixteen—went on strike, Jones coordinated a dramatic protest. She led the youthful workers on a 125-mile march from their workplace to the home of President Theodore Roosevelt (1858–1919; president from 1901–09) on Long Island, near New York City. Many journalists accompanied the marchers on their journey and provided extensive media coverage of the event. After a final march through the streets of New York City, Jones and a group of children proceeded to Roosevelt's home. The president, however, declined to meet with them.

Although the march produced no immediate results, the following year the state of Pennsylvania passed child labor restriction laws. New York, New Jersey, and a handful of other states passed child labor laws within the next few years. It was not until 1938, however, that Congress passed the Fair Labor Standards Act, abolishing child labor throughout the United States.

Undeterred by arrests, jailings, and personal attacks

From 1900 until 1920 Jones continued to travel around the country supporting striking workers. Jones was as deeply despised by law enforcement authorities as she was loved by miners. In the media Jones was called "the most dangerous woman in America."

The fiery speeches Jones gave in defiance of police orders landed her in jail several times. In 1913, for example, when a strike in West Virginia turned violent, an eighty-two-year-old Jones was convicted in a military court of conspiracy to commit murder (she had been forced by police into an area in which martial law had been declared and arrested). Jones was sentenced to twenty years in prison. After spending three months in solitary confinement, however, the governor responded to public outcry on Jones's behalf and granted her a pardon. The following year, while rallying miners in Colorado, Jones was held without charge for twenty-six days in the cellar of a county courthouse.

Among the many personal attacks Jones's enemies launched at her was the charge of being "unladylike." To that accusation Jones replied, in her typically defiant manner, "A lady is the last thing on earth I want to be." She went on to explain that "capitalists sidetrack the women into clubs and make ladies of them. Nobody wants a lady, they want women. Ladies are parlor parasites."

Settles in Silver Springs

In 1920 the ninety-year-old Jones, crippled by rheumatoid arthritis, finally retired from rabble-rousing. Having no family or savings of her own, Jones was taken in by a retired mine worker and his wife in Silver Springs, Maryland. There she received many visitors and made occasional speeches.

On May 1, 1930—Jones's one-hundredth birthday (or so she claimed) —she was carried outside for a celebration in her honor. There she made a speech that was broadcast on nation-wide radio. Her plea for workers' rights, and her denunciation of exploitation by wealthy owners, was every bit as passionate as it had been in earlier years.

Buried in Mount Olive Miners Cemetery

Jones died on November 1, 1930, in Silver Springs. As she had requested, she was buried in Miners Cemetery—the only union-owned cemetery in the United States—in Mount Olive, Illinois. Her funeral attracted thousands of mourners, many of whom were mine workers. Today a large granite monument with statues of two mine workers marks Jones's grave.

Sources

Books

Button, John. *The Radicalism Handbook.* London, England: Cassell, 1995, pp. 196–97.

Fetherling, Dale. *Mother Jones: The Miners' Angel.* Carbondale, IL: Southern Illinois University Press, 1974.

Jones, Mary Harris. *The Autobiography of Mother Jones,* 3rd ed. Chicago: Charles H. Kerr Publishing Company, 1976.

Josephson, Judith Pinkerton. *Mother Jones: Fierce Fighter for Workers' Rights.* Minneapolis: Lerner Publications Company, 1997.

"Mother Jones." *Contemporary Heroes and Heroines.* Vol. 2. Edited by Deborah Gillan Straub. Detroit: Gale Research, 1992.

Articles

Mackey, Heather. "Ronnie Gilbert: Resurrecting Mother Jones." *American Theatre.* July-August 1993: 47+.

A Tribute to "Mother" Jones

The following poem, whose author remains anonymous, was written as a tribute to "Mother" Jones:

The world today is mourning
The death of Mother Jones;
Grief and sorrow hover
Over the miners' homes;
This grand old champion of labor
Has gone to a better land,
But the hard-working miners,
They miss her guiding hand.

Through the hills and over the valleys,
In every mining town,
Mother Jones was ready to help them—
She never turned them down.
In front with the striking miners
She always could be found,
She fought for right and justice,
She took a noble stand.

With a spirit strong and fearless
She hated that which was wrong;
She never gave up fighting,
Until her breath was gone.
May the workers all get together
To carry out her plan,
And bring back better conditions
To every laboring man.

Florence Kelley

Born September 12, 1859
Philadelphia, Pennsylvania
Died February 17, 1932
Philadelphia, Pennsylvania

Child-welfare activist, workplace reformer, women's rights activist, and lawyer

Florence Kelley devoted her life to the passage of laws that would keep children out of the workplace and make work more humane for adults. Kelley summarized her strategy for social change as "investigate, educate, legislate, and enforce."

Florence Kelley.
Courtesy of the Library of Congress.

Florence Kelley spent the better part of four decades campaigning for the abolition of child labor. In 1891, with three children of her own, Kelley moved into Chicago's famous settlement house and center for social reformers, Hull House. There she gathered information on wages and working conditions for adults and children in the community. Her report inspired the Illinois state legislature to pass workplace safety laws and to hire Kelley as chief factory inspector for the state. Kelley later became secretary-general of the National Consumers' League, an organization that used the buying power of consumers to press for fair working conditions in factories. In 1938—six years after Kelley's death—Congress passed the Fair Labor Standards Act, abolishing child labor and setting maximum hours and minimum wage for all working adults.

Father was a social reformer

Kelley was born into a politically active Quaker family on September 12, 1859, in Philadelphia, Pennsylvania. She was greatly influenced by her father, William Darrow Kelley, who served in the U.S. House of Representatives for twenty years. William Kelley was an abolitionist (a person who fought for an end to slavery) and later a radical reconstructionist (a person who advocated equal rights for African Americans after the Civil War, 1861–65).

William Kelley was a proponent of woman suffrage (the right to vote), as well. At the request of Susan B. Anthony—his friend and famed women's rights activist (1820–1906; see entry on **Elizabeth Cady Stanton**)—he introduced a woman suffrage amendment into Congress in 1869. The amendment failed that year and every subsequent year until its adoption in 1920.

Congressman Kelley was also concerned about the consequences of child labor. When Florence was twelve years old her father took her into factories so she could witness the conditions that poor children were forced to endure. Florence would never forget that experience.

Studies politics, economics, and law

Kelley attended the Quaker-run Friends' Central School in Philadelphia, but she frequently missed classes due to illness. She supplemented her education by reading every book in her father's library. Kelley attended a high school for young women, then enrolled in Cornell University in New York. Again, due to illness, she only attended classes intermittently. Kelley studied law, economics, politics, French, German, Latin, and American history. She graduated with honors in 1882, six years after she had begun, with a bachelor of arts degree.

Kelley spent the next year teaching night classes to working women in Philadelphia. She then traveled to the University of Zurich, in Switzerland, for graduate training in government and law.

Meets husband and prominent socialists in Zurich

In Zurich Kelley met a Russian medical student named Lazare Wischnewetzky; the two were married in 1884. She also met a number of prominent European socialists (people who believe that the means of production should not be controlled by owners, but by the community as a whole), including German economist and author Friedrich Engels (1820–1895; see box in **Karl Marx** entry). Kelley maintained a long correspondence with Engels and in 1887 translated into English his book *The Condition of the Working Class in England in 1844.*

Returns to New York and ends marriage

Kelley returned to the United States in 1886 with her husband and infant son Nicholas. They lived in New York City, where Kelley became active in the Socialist Labor Party. In 1887 Kelley authored an essay explaining, in simple terms, the socialist theory of German social and economic theorist **Karl Marx** (1818–1883; see entry). Two years later she wrote a pamphlet denouncing child labor—a topic that would become her life's work—called "Our Toiling Children."

While in New York, Kelley's marriage became strained. Her husband's medical practice was unsuccessful and the family's bills accumulated. Wischnewetzky responded to the stress of the situation by becoming physically abusive. In 1891 the couple divorced. By that time they had three children, ages six, five, and four.

Moves into Hull House

Following her divorce, Kelley moved with her children to Chicago, Illinois. They took up residence in Hull House—a settlement house where exciting social reform work was taking place. (A settlement house is an organization devoted to the improvement of neighborhood life.) Hull House was a community center, neighborhood association, and cultural and educational institution in a working-class section of Chicago. It was founded in 1889 by pioneering social worker and advocate for the poor **Jane Addams** (1860–1935; see entry).

Hull House attracted the attention of prominent American social reformers, several of whom took up residence there. The reformers worked for antipoverty measures, the rights of women in the workplace, an end to child labor, the establishment of juvenile protection agencies, safety measures in factories, and the right of women to vote. They also helped with the formation of labor unions. Kelley, with her extensive education, passion for justice, and outgoing personality, was a welcome addition to the Hull House circle of activists.

Report inspires passage of Illinois labor act

After moving into Hull House, Kelley found work inspecting sweatshops (small, unregulated textile factories in which workers—many of them young girls—are paid low wages and toil in unpleasant and often dangerous conditions) in the clothing industry, as a special agent for the Illinois Bureau of Labor Statistics. During that time Kelley also investigated the living and working conditions of people living in the slums of Chicago. She recorded information about the occupations and wages of adults, and whether the children worked or went to school. She concluded in her report that a large proportion of children under the age of fourteen were working full time and not attending school, and that both adults and children worked in unsafe conditions, for long hours and poor wages.

Kelley presented her report to the Illinois state legislature and lectured about her findings at churches, meetings, and clubs. In 1893, shortly after the presentation of Kelley's report, Illinois lawmakers voted to abolish child labor (for children younger than fourteen), restrict the workday for children and women to eight hours, and establish a state factory inspection department. Kelley was named chief factory inspector for the state.

Works as chief factory inspector and earns law degree

In her position as chief factory inspector, Kelley stretched a small departmental budget to provide a free medical examination center for working children. She also visited more than a thousand factories during a smallpox epidemic, searching for contaminated garments. (Smallpox is a highly contagious, potentially deadly disease. It produces pus-filled scabs that often leave permanent scars or pits.) Kelley ordered all contaminated garments to be discarded to prevent the spread of the virus to workers or people who would buy the clothing.

On at least one occasion Kelley was unable to obtain the legal assistance necessary to challenge a factory that was in violation of labor laws. That frustration led her to attend law school. In 1895 Kelley completed her law degree at Northwestern University in Evanston, Illinois. That same year, how-

Julia Lathrop, Child Welfare Social Worker

Julia Lathrop (1858–1932) was a colleague of Florence Kelley's and one of the Hull House social reformers. In 1912 Lathrop became the first person to head the United States Children's Bureau—a child welfare agency established largely through the lobbying efforts of Kelley.

Lathrop was born in Rockford, Illinois, and graduated from Vassar College in Poughkeepsie, New York, in 1880. She arrived at Hull House in 1890 (the year before Kelley) and remained there for twenty years. During that time, as the first female member of the Illinois State Board of Charities, Lathrop campaigned for the removal of mentally disabled people from poorhouses. She argued for the establishment of facilities at which those people, labeled "insane," could receive proper treatment. Lathrop also fought for the hiring of female doctors and nurses in state hospitals. Her advocacy for the establishment of the first juvenile court in the United States met with success in 1900 (prior to that time juveniles had been held in the same facilities, and judged by the same rules, as adults).

As head of the Children's Bureau, Lathrop conducted studies on child labor, infant mortality, juvenile delinquency, and

Julia Lathrop, Jane Addams, and Mary McDowell. *Reproduced by permission of Corbis Corporation.*

the social stigma attached to children of unmarried parents. Lathrop also lobbied for federally funded health programs for mothers and children. Her efforts met with success in 1921 with the Sheppard-Towner Act, which incorporated child and maternal health programs into the Social Security Act. After ten years with the Children's Bureau, Lathrop resigned and started working with the Child Welfare Committee of the League of Nations (The League of Nations was the forerunner organization to the United Nations).

ever, her work suffered a setback: the law restricting the workday of women and minors to eight hours was declared unconstitutional by the Illinois Supreme Court.

Heads National Consumers' League

In 1897 the liberal governor of Illinois, John Peter Altgeld, lost reelection, and Kelley was removed from her post of chief factory inspector. Two years later Kelley became secretary-general of the National Consumers' League (NCL)—an agency she helped found that lobbied for protective labor legislation for women and children. Kelley moved to New York City, where the NCL was headquartered, and took up residence in the Henry Street settlement house.

In Kelley's position at the helm of the NCL, which she held for the rest of her life, she traveled widely throughout the United States. Kelley helped establish sixty-four local branches of the organization and lectured about the need for laws governing workers' rights (including minimum wage and maximum work hours, safety in factories, and the abolition of child labor). Kelley urged consumers to buy no products except those bearing the Consumers' League label. The label was only given to producers who did not employ child labor and who treated workers fairly.

Kelley also advocated the establishment of a national Children's Bureau—an agency that would promote the general welfare of children. To that end, Kelley in 1905 published *Some Ethical Gains through Legislation,* which emphasized the need to abolish child labor, give women the vote, and pass federal wage and hours laws. Kelley's efforts paid off in 1912 with the establishment of the United States Children's Bureau (see box on Julia Lathrop).

Setbacks during the 1920s

In response to the increasing influence of socialism throughout the early 1900s and during World War I (1914–18), the United States experienced a conservative backlash in the 1920s. Social reformers such as Kelley, Addams, and other Hull House members were labeled "communists" and shunned in the press.

During the 1920s Kelley witnessed the dismantling of much of the worker-protection legislation she had worked so hard to achieve. For example, the federal government funding for maternity and infant health programs, begun in 1920, was revoked in 1929. In 1918 and in 1922 the Supreme Court struck down two separate laws banning child labor and in 1923 overturned the minimum wage law for women. Although Kelley had been able to push the Child Labor Amendment (a constitutional amendment abolishing child labor) through both houses of Congress in 1924, the amendment failed to receive ratification by the required three-quarters of state legislatures.

Life's work fulfilled after death

Five years after Kelley's death, during the throes of the Great Depression (the worst economic recession ever to hit the United States, from 1929 through 1939), the political tide shifted in favor of social reform. In 1937 the Supreme Court reversed its 1923 stand and upheld the minimum wage law for women that had been established in Washington, D.C. An even more significant endorsement of Kelley's work came the next year when Congress passed the Fair Labor Standards Act. That legislation abolished child labor and set maximum hours and minimum wage for all working adults.

Sources

Books
"Florence Kelley." *Gale Encyclopedia of U.S. Economic History.* Farmington Hills, MI: The Gale Group, 1999.

Goldmark, Josephine. *Impatient Crusader: Florence Kelley's Life Story.* Urbana: University of Illinois Press, 1953.

Saller, Carol. *Florence Kelley.* Minneapolis: Carolrhoda Books, Inc., 1997.

Articles
Sklar, Kathryn Kish. "Florence Kelley." *The Reader's Companion to American History.* Annual 1991: 610+.

Martin Luther King, Jr.

**Born January 15, 1929
Atlanta, Georgia
Died April 4, 1968
Memphis, Tennessee**

**African American civil rights leader
and minister**

Martin Luther King, Jr., spent the final decade of his life in relentless pursuit of racial equality and social justice. As president of the Southern Christian Leadership Conference, King led a peaceful movement for racial equality and justice in the southern United States. With his gift for impassioned and inspirational speech, King convinced ordinary people to take courageous actions they would have never before imagined possible. In a span of ten years, King and his fellow civil rights activists transformed the American South from a bastion of white supremacy into a region where African Americans had the right to vote, the right to attend integrated schools, and the right to take any seat on a public bus.

> "For years now, I have heard the word 'Wait.' It rings in the ears of every Negro with piercing familiarity. This 'Wait' has almost always meant 'Never.'"
>
> *Martin Luther King, Jr., in "Letter from a Birmingham Jail"*

Religious upbringing and education

King was born in 1929 in Atlanta, Georgia, into a religious family. King's father, Martin Luther King, Sr., was the pastor of Atlanta's Ebenezer Baptist Church. King's mother, Alberta (Williams) King, was a schoolteacher and a minister's daughter.

Although King had a religious upbringing and religious education, he originally intended to pursue a career in law or medicine. After graduating from Booker T. Washington High School at the age of fifteen, King continued his studies at Morehouse College in Atlanta. During the course of his studies, King decided to become a minister. He gradiated from Morehouse with a bachelor of arts degree in 1948, then enrolled in Crozer Theological Seminary in Chester, Pennsylvania. King, one of just six African American students in a class with a hundred whites, was elected president of the student body. He graduated at the top of his class with a bachelor of divinity degree from Crozer in 1951, then went to Boston University, in Massachusetts, to pursue his doctorate.

Discovers Gandhi's teachings

While in Boston, King discovered the teachings of **Mohandas Gandhi** (1869–1948; see entry), the leader of India's independence movement against Great Britain. Gandhi advocated nonviolence—the use of moral persuasion, not weapons, to defeat one's enemies. King later applied Gandhi's philosophy of nonviolence to the civil rights movement.

During his years at Boston University, King met a music student named Coretta Scott (1927–). The two were married by King's father in 1953. The newlywed Kings then moved to Montgomery, Alabama, where Martin had been offered the ministry of the Dexter Avenue Baptist Church.

The Montgomery Bus Boycott

King's first experience with social justice movements came in 1955, during the Montgomery, Alabama, bus boycott. The boycott had been sparked by Rosa Parks's (1913– ; see box in **Highlander Center** entry) refusal to move to the back of a city bus, and subsequent arrest, on December 1, 1955. Two local organizations—the National Association for the Advancement of Colored People (NAACP) and the Women's Political Council (WPC) proposed that African Americans boycott city buses to protest racist policies and Parks's arrest.

Then twenty-six years old, King was selected by a group of African American ministers and community members to be president of the Montgomery Improvement Association (MIA)—the organization that had been created to coordinate the boycott.

At the conclusion of the first day, King stood on the pulpit of his overflowing church and made the case for continuing the boycott. "There comes a time that people get tired," proclaimed King. "We are here this evening to say to those who have mistreated us for so long that we are tired—tired of being . . . kicked about by the brutal feet of oppression. When the history books are written in future generations the historians will pause and say, 'There lived a great people—a black people—who injected new meaning and dignity into the veins of civilization.' That is our challenge and our overwhelming responsibility."

The decision was made to continue the boycott until African American riders would no longer be forced to give up their seats to whites. The boycotters also demanded more respectful treatment of African Americans by bus drivers and the hiring of black drivers. The boycott lasted 382 days and was ultimately successful. On December 20, 1956, the Montgomery City Lines bus company was served with a court order to abandon its policy of racial segregation.

The founding of the SCLC

As the bus boycott came to a close, King was approached by **Ella Baker** (1903–1986; see entry), a fifty-two-year-old civil rights activist from New York, with the idea of forming a permanent organization of African American ministers to coordinate civil rights activities in the South. After some debate, King agreed. On January 10 and 11, 1957, sixty-five African American ministers from eleven southern states came to King's father's church, the Ebenezer Baptist Church in Atlanta, Georgia, to found the Southern Christian Leadership Conference (SCLC). The group selected King as the SCLC's first president. The SCLC quickly rose to prominence as the South's most respected civil rights organization.

King then traveled throughout the South, supporting local civil rights struggles and giving speeches. In 1958 King accepted an invitation to celebrate the independence of the African country of Ghana. The following year King visited

India, to reaffirm his belief in Gandhian nonviolence. King moved to Atlanta in 1960, to devote more time to the SCLC and to serve alongside his father as pastor of the Ebenezer Baptist Church.

The Birmingham protest campaign

In 1963 King and the SCLC sought to desegregate Birmingham, Alabama, which according to King was "probably the most thoroughly segregated city in the United States." The SCLC decided on a course of action including boycotts of selected downtown department stores (those that had segregated lunch counters or otherwise discriminated against African Americans), marches, and demonstrations. They demanded the desegregation of downtown lunch counters and stores and an end to discrimination in employment.

On April 12 King and SCLC vice president Ralph Abernathy (1926–1990) led a march to city hall. The protesters, singing hymns, were halted by police and arrested. King spent a week in jail, during which time he wrote his famous "Letter from a Birmingham Jail" (see box).

On April 20 King and Abernathy were freed on bond. The following week, two thousand children marched in the streets for civil rights. On the second day of the demonstration, Birmingham police clubbed the children, set dogs upon them, and blasted them with firehoses. Outraged by the attack on the youngsters, thousands of people demonstrated in Birmingham, and more than two thousand were arrested.

The disturbances finally brought Birmingham merchants and lawmakers to the table. On May 10, 1963, an accord was reached that promised an end to segregation in downtown stores (including lunch counters, rest rooms, fitting rooms, and drinking fountains) and the employment of African Americans in clerical and sales positions. King declared the accord to be "the most magnificent victory for justice we've seen in the Deep South."

The March on Washington

In June 1963 President John F. Kennedy (1917–1963; president 1961–63) proposed a sweeping civil rights bill that

Letter from a Birmingham Jail

While sitting in isolation in a Birmingham jail in April 1963 for his activities in the Birmingham desegregation campaign, King read a statement by a group of white religious leaders in the local paper. The clergymen called the Birmingham demonstrations "unwise and untimely" and stated: "We do not believe that these days of new hope are days when extreme measures are needed in Birmingham." (The "new hope" referred to a newly elected mayor and city council.)

King wrote a response—his famous "Letter from a Birmingham Jail"—on the margins of newspaper and sheets of toilet paper. He then had the letter smuggled out of jail. King's letter was originally published in the form of a pamphlet distributed by a Quaker organization called the **American Friends Service Committee** (see entry). It was reprinted in dozens of newspapers and magazines around the country.

"I have yet to engage in a direct action campaign," wrote King, "that was well-timed in the view of those who have not suffered from the disease of segregation. For years now, I have heard the word 'Wait.' It rings in the ears of every Negro with piercing familiarity. This 'Wait' has almost always meant 'Never.'"

would outlaw segregation of all public accommodations, speed up school desegregation, and make it easier for African Americans to register to vote. King joined with **A. Philip Randolph** (see entry) and other African American labor leaders, who were already planning a march on Washington, D.C., for jobs and justice, to coordinate a massive show of support for the proposed legislation.

On the morning of August 28, 1963, 250,000 people descended upon Washington in the largest protest march to that date. Several civil rights leaders delivered speeches at the Lincoln Memorial. The speech that moved the audience more than any other that day was the final one, King's "I Have a Dream."

"I have a dream," pronounced King, "that one day on the red hills of Georgia the sons of former slaves and the sons of former slave owners will be able to sit down together at the table of brotherhood. I have a dream that my four little children will one day live in a nation where they will not be judged by the color of their skin but the content of their character . . . "

At the end of 1963 King was chosen as "Man of the Year" by *Time* magazine. The following year King received an even higher honor—the Nobel Peace Prize.

The crusade for voting rights

Even after the passage of the 1964 Civil Rights Act, it was still very difficult for African Americans to register to vote in the South. King and other civil rights leaders believed that stronger federal legislation was needed to outlaw the variety of practices used by racist officials to keep African Americans from voting.

To draw attention to their cause, civil rights leaders organized a major voting-rights campaign in Selma, Alabama. Selma provided a glaring example of African Americans' denial of the right to vote: while the majority of the citizens of Selma were black, less than 3 percent of African American adults were registered to vote.

King arrived in Selma on January 2, 1965, and declared, "We are not asking, we are demanding the ballot." Throughout the month of January, more than two thousand people marched to the courthouse and unsuccessfully attempted to register to vote. When the protesters refused to leave, they were arrested. In the first three days of February, King was among the more than 1,500 people arrested at the courthouse.

The Selma to Montgomery march

In early March the SCLC planned a fifty-four-mile-long protest march from Selma to the state capital of Montgomery. In Montgomery the marchers would present a list of grievances to the governor. The march began three times before marchers were finally allowed to proceed to Montgomery. On the first attempt, known as "Bloody Sunday" (March 7), the marchers were attacked by police and state troopers on the Edmund Pettus Bridge at the edge of Selma. On the second attempt, marchers encountered troops and turned around on the bridge without incident.

On March 25, over three thousand participants gathered for their third and final attempt. When the procession reached Montgomery four days later, the number of marchers had reached twenty-five thousand. King gave a triumphant speech on the steps of the state capitol before a crowd of fifty thousand people.

The events in Selma convinced President Lyndon B. Johnson (1908–1973) to introduce a voting rights bill in Congress. The 1965 Voting Rights Act, passed on August 6, 1965, outlawed all practices used to deny African Americans the right to vote and empowered federal registrars to register African American voters.

King visits riot-torn Watts

King visited the Watts section of Los Angeles, California, in August 1965, shortly after six days of rioting had reduced the forty-five-square-mile area to ruins. Watts was one of many African American inner-city ghettoes in the northern and western United States that exploded in anger between the years 1964 and 1968.

King learned that while southern African Americans had been victimized by legally sanctioned racial segregation, northern and western African Americans suffered from oppressive poverty, overcrowding, and discrimination in housing and employment. King's Watts visit led him to the conclusion that racial justice could only be achieved by a drastic change in the nation's economic structure.

The SCLC's "Campaign to End Slums" in Chicago

In January 1966 King and his staff launched the "Campaign to End Slums" in Chicago, Illinois. The group chose Chicago, the nation's second-largest city, for the campaign because the one-quarter of the city's residents who were African American faced relentless poverty and discrimination. Through a variety of segregation practices, African Americans in Chicago were confined to the ghetto.

King and his aides were optimistic at the start of the campaign. Nevertheless, after nine months the campaign

ended in failure. King found that he did not have as great a following among northern African Americans as he did among southern African Americans, and that his Chicago constituency was not devoted to nonviolence. King was also deterred by the extreme racial hatred exhibited by white Chicagoans and the tactics of Mayor Richard Daley. Daley, whose political machine controlled all city services from trash removal to public housing to welfare, denied essential services to residents who participated in the campaign.

King, anxious to end the campaign, announced on August 26 that a settlement had been reached. City officials and real estate agents pledged an end to housing discrimination and King agreed to end the demonstrations. King and his aides then left Chicago. The pledges of city officials and real estate agents, however, went unfulfilled.

Champions the rights of poor people

After his experience in Chicago, King made his priority

the rights of poor people of all races. At the same time, King became an outspoken opponent of the Vietnam War (1954–75). He not only opposed the war because of his pacifist views but also because African Americans were dying in disproportionate numbers, and spending for the war had detracted from federal antipoverty programs.

In the fall of 1967 King began organizing a Poor People's March on Washington, to be held the following spring. King envisioned a march in which thousands of poor people of all races would come to the nation's capital, set up a tent city, and lobby legislators for programs that would expand economic opportunity.

King was prevented from leading the Poor People's March by an assassin's bullet (see below). After King's death, SCLC vice president Ralph Abernathy took over the project reins. In May 1968, the Poor People's March arrived in Washington, D.C., and set up a tent city, called Resurrection City. The whole affair received scant mention in the press. By late June, when ceaseless rains had turned the tent city into a swamp, organizers ended the campaign.

The final days of King's life

On March 28, 1968, King arrived in Memphis, Tennessee, to aid striking African American sanitation workers. King led a protest march to city hall in support of the workers' demands for better wages and working conditions. Along the march route, a riot broke out that left sixty people injured and a sixteen-year-old boy dead. Despite having received several death threats, King vowed to stay in Memphis until he could lead a nonviolent demonstration.

On April 3 King addressed a gathering at the Mason Temple Church. "We've got some difficult days ahead," stated King. "But it really doesn't matter to me now. Because I've been to the mountaintop. . . . 'Mine eyes have seen the glory of the coming of the Lord.'"

King's words in the pulpit foretold his life's tragic ending. The next morning, April 4, 1968, while standing on the balcony of the Lorraine Hotel, King was shot and killed by an assassin named James Earl Ray. King was carried to his final resting place, near the Ebenezer Baptist Church in Atlanta, on a mule-drawn cart. Eighteen years after King's death a national holiday was established in his honor.

Sources

Books

African Americans: Voices of Triumph: Perseverance. Alexandria, VA: Time-Life Books, 1993.

Carson, Clayborne, and Peter Holloran, eds. *A Knock at Midnight: Inspiration from the Great Sermons of Reverend Martin Luther King, Jr.* New York: Warner Books, Inc., 1998.

Garrow, David J. *Protest at Selma: Martin Luther King, Jr., and the Voting Rights Act of 1965.* New Haven, CT: Yale University Press, 1978.

King, Martin Luther, Jr. *A Testament of Hope: The Essential Writings of Martin Luther King, Jr.* San Francisco: Harper and Row, Publishers, 1986.

Levine, Michael L. *African Americans and Civil Rights from 1619 to the Present.* Phoenix, AZ: Oryx Press, 1996.

Patterson, Lillie. *Martin Luther King, Jr., and the Freedom Movement.* New York: Facts on File, 1989.

Robinson, Jo Ann Gibson. *The Montgomery Bus Boycott and the Women Who Started It.* Knoxville: University of Tennessee Press, 1987.

Salmond, John A. *My Mind Set on Freedom: A History of the Civil Rights Movement, 1954–1968.* Chicago: Ivan R. Dee, 1997.

Weisbrot, Robert. *Marching toward Freedom, 1957–1965.* New York: Chelsea House Publishers, 1994.

Williams, Juan. *Eyes on the Prize: America's Civil Rights Years, 1954–1965.* New York: Penguin Books, 1987.

Winona LaDuke

**Born 1959
Los Angeles, California**

**Environmentalist, Native American
rights activist, and writer**

Winona LaDuke is one of the nation's foremost Native American environmental activists. She combines her mission of protecting the land with the promotion of economic and cultural viability of Indian communities. As LaDuke stated in a 1995 interview with *The Progressive,* the focus of her work is to change society "from the synthetic reality of consumption and expendability to the natural reality of conservation and harmony."

"Our land reaffirms us, makes us who we are, gives us the instructions to form our lives."

Winona LaDuke, Harper's Bazaar, *1994*

Raised to respect Indian heritage

Winona LaDuke was born in 1959 in an Indian neighborhood in East Los Angeles, California. Her parents were Vincent LaDuke, an Ojibwa Indian, and Betty Bernstein, a Jewish woman. Vincent was an Indian-rights activists and an actor who had small roles in numerous films. Betty was an artist from New York City.

Both of LaDuke's parents were supporters of human rights—especially Native American rights. LaDuke on several occasions missed school to attend civil rights and antiwar marches with her parents.

Winona LaDuke.
Reproduced by permission of AP/Wide World Photos.

315

LaDuke's parents raised her to respect Native American cultural traditions. As a youth, LaDuke made several visits to her father's childhood home—the White Earth Indian Reservation in rural northern Minnesota. Her father took her to cultural and spiritual gatherings called powwows. "I was never told to go out and make money," stated LaDuke in a 1995 interview, "but to do the right thing."

When LaDuke was five years old, her parents divorced. LaDuke then moved with her mother to Ashland, Oregon. Living in a mostly white neighborhood and attending a mostly white school, LaDuke for the first time experienced racial discrimination. As she grew older she learned that racism was not just a characteristic of her community, but was widespread throughout the United States.

Protests environmental damage to Indian lands

LaDuke did well in school, despite the cruel treatment she received from her white classmates. Upon graduating from high school in 1976 she was offered, and accepted, a scholarship to Harvard University in Cambridge, Massachusetts. It was at Harvard that LaDuke met young Native Americans involved in various Native American causes. During her student years LaDuke participated in a number of activist groups.

The issue that made the greatest impact on LaDuke was the environmental destruction of Indian reservation lands, particularly at the hands of government agencies and corporations. During one summer vacation LaDuke traveled to Arizona to participate in a campaign to stop the mining of uranium on Navajo lands.

Also while a student LaDuke worked for the International Indian Treaty Council. She traveled to a United Nations conference in Geneva, Switzerland, as a representative of the Council and testified about the devastation of Indian lands resulting from strip mining, toxic waste dumping, and nuclear weapons testing.

Moves to White Earth Indian Reservation

After graduating from Harvard with a degree in native economic development, LaDuke went on to earn a master's degree from Antioch College in Yellow Springs, Ohio. In 1982 she made a homecoming of sorts, to the White Earth Reservation. LaDuke spent one year working as the principal of the reservation high school, after which she quit to devote all her time to the issue of land restoration.

LaDuke learned that the White Earth reservation had been chiseled away, one parcel at a time, since its establishment by treaty in 1867. Originally encompassing 837,000 acres of forests, wetlands, and lakes, the reservation had been reduced to 7,890 acres by 1934. Through a series of questionable real estate transactions and government repossession of land on which taxes were owed, the land had ended up in the hands of lumber companies and white farmers and ranchers. "Our land reaffirms us," stated LaDuke in a *Harper's Bazaar* article of 1994, "makes us who we are, gives us the instructions to form our lives. If you lose control of your land, you lose your essence."

LaDuke organized a group of White Earth residents to file suit against the U.S. government in an attempt to reclaim the land they had lost. They claimed that U.S. government policies not only failed to protect the land, but actually encouraged its transfer to non-Indians. LaDuke was never able to present the evidence she had gathered because the suit was thrown out of court.

In 1986 LaDuke met Cree activist Randy Kapashesit, from Moose Factory, Canada, at a Native American conference in Toronto, Canada. The two wed and had two children. Neither LaDuke nor Kapashesit were able to move from their respective communities, so they maintained a long-distance relationship. That arrangement proved too stressful and they separated in 1992.

Founds White Earth Land Recovery Project

After her initial failure to reclaim land through a lawsuit, LaDuke came up with another strategy: she formed an organization to publicize the loss of Ojibwa land and to win it back. In 1986 LaDuke won the Reebok Human Rights Award, which included a $20 thousand prize. She used the prize money to establish the White Earth Land Recovery Project (WELRP). As director of the project, LaDuke raises money to buy back parcels of land for White Earth and to finance land

AIM Activist Anna Mae Aquash

Anna Mae Aquash (1945–1976) was a Canadian-born Native American rights activist. As a young adult, Aquash worked as an educator and social service provider for young Native Americans in New England. Aquash's involvement with the **American Indian Movement** (AIM; see entry) began in 1970, when she participated in an AIM-sponsored Thanksgiving Day protest near Plymouth Rock—the site of the original pilgrims' landing. (AIM is a militant Indian-rights group, founded in 1968, that fights for the return of tribal lands, enforcement of government treaties, respect for the human rights of Native Americans, and greater economic opportunities for Indians.)

In 1973 Aquash left her home and job and headed to South Dakota to devote all her time and energy to the pursuit of Indian rights. Aquash's destination was the Pine Ridge Reservation, where her AIM friends had taken over the village of Wounded Knee. (Wounded Knee was the site of the 1890 massacre of over 150—some estimates place the number as high as 370—Indian men, women, and children by U.S. military forces.) The modern-day Wounded Knee occupation had been undertaken in protest of the corrupt practices of tribal chairman Richard Wilson and the brutality of his police force. Aquash helped build bunkers and took her turn on night patrols. She also sneaked

claim suits. She also solicits donations of reservation land which is held by non-Native Americans.

As of 1995, LaDuke had recovered more than one thousand acres of White Earth land—including several acres of burial grounds. Her goal is to increase the size of the reservation to thirty thousand acres by the year 2010.

In addition to reclaiming land, the WELRP sponsors economic and cultural initiatives. For example, WELRP runs an organic raspberry farm, a maple sugar production facility, and a wild rice production and marketing operation. WELRP also provides Ojibwa language classes to reservation children, beginning in preschool, and to their families. LaDuke recognizes that few young people in recent years have learned their native tongue and hopes that the language instruction will help keep the Ojibwa language alive.

food and medical supplies into Wounded Knee at night.

In 1974 Aquash moved to St. Paul, Minnesota, to work in AIM's national headquarters. She also established the West Coast office of AIM in Los Angeles, California. Aquash's rise within the ranks of AIM came to the attention of COINTELPRO operatives in the FBI. COINTELPRO, which stands for Counter Intelligence Program, was a secret FBI operation in the 1960s and 1970s that gathered information on and attempted to destroy the anti-Vietnam War movement, the civil rights movement, and militant organizations of people of color.

In late 1975 Aquash was pressured by FBI agents to give testimony against fellow AIM-member Leonard Peltier, who had been charged in the shooting death of two FBI agents. When Aquash claimed she had no information about the incident, she was told by FBI agent David Price she would be "dead within a year."

On February 24, 1976, Aquash's body was found by a Lakota cattle rancher. The corpse was partially deteriorated, indicating that it had been there for quite some time. An autopsy revealed that Aquash had been shot in the back of the head at point-blank range. While Aquash's murder remains officially unsolved, Native American activists continue to suspect the FBI.

Becomes cochair of Indigenous Women's Network

In 1989 LaDuke organized and became cochairperson of the Indigenous Women's Network (IWN)—a funding organization for Native American women's community groups. The IWN provides grants to groups that are working to strengthen cultural traditions and to protect the environment.

LaDuke initiated a major fund-raising campaign for IWN in 1995, involving a series of concerts by the band Indigo Girls. The concert tour, called "Honor the Earth," traveled through twenty-seven cities and raised nearly $250 thousand. That spring LaDuke led an IWN delegation to the United Nations Women's Conference in Beijing, China. LaDuke addressed the conference on behalf of IWN.

Runs as Green Party vice-presidential candidate

In 1996 LaDuke ran for vice president of the United States on the Green Party ticket. (The Green Party is a political organization that promotes environmentalism, women's rights, and workers' rights.) The party's presidential candidate was consumer advocate **Ralph Nader** (1934– ; see entry). Nader and LaDuke appeared on the ballot in thirty states and garnered approximately two percent of the vote in those states. Nader and LaDuke ran again on the Green Party ticket in 2000.

In 1997 LaDuke authored a novel titled *Last Standing Woman*. The novel recounts the lives of seven generations of Ojibwa Indians. It begins with their first contact with white people and ends in the 1990s, after a fictitious battle similar to the 1973 occupation of Wounded Knee (see box on Anna Mae Aquash).

In addition to her work on the White Earth Reservation and with Native American women, LaDuke lectures at college campuses and is on the board of directors of Greenpeace (an environmental protection organization). She also serves as the environmental program officer of the Seventh Generation Fund. LaDuke, as described in a 1995 *Progressive* article, "has an incredible drive to get things done" and "exudes a great personal warmth."

Sources

Books

Brand, Johanna. *The Life and Death of Anna Mae Aquash.* Toronto: James Lorimer and Company Publishers, 1993.

Engelbert, Phillis. *American Civil Rights Biographies.* Farmington Hills, MI: U•X•L, 1999, pp. 23–30.

Sonneborn, Liz. *A to Z of Native American Women.* New York: Facts on File, 1998, pp. 85–87.

"Winona LaDuke." *Newsmakers 1995.* Issue 4. Detroit: Gale Research Inc., 1995.

Articles

Barbieri, Susan M. "Winona LaDuke Fights to Preserve Indian Culture, Safeguard the Environment and Reclaim Tribal Lands." *Knight-Ridder/Tribune News Service.* June 14, 1995.

Bogenschutz, Debbie. Review of "Last Standing Woman." *Library Journal.* November 15, 1997: 77.

Bowmaster, Jon. "Earth of a Nation." *Harper's Bazaar.* April 1994: 101–2.

Rosen, Marjorie. "Friend of the Earth." *People Weekly.* November 28, 1994: 165+.

Sonya, Paul, and Robert Perkinson. "Winona LaDuke." (Interview.) *The Progressive.* October 1995: 36+.

Other Sources

"Winona LaDuke: Sustainable Wisdom." EMI Sustainable Environment Series. BMC Media Services, University of Michigan, 1999. Video-recording.

Felicia Langer

Born December 3, 1930
Tarnow, Poland

Israeli human rights attorney

Felicia Langer is an Israeli lawyer who, after becoming aware of injustices committed against Palestinians, decided to focus her legal career on their defense. Her service to Palestinian clients began in 1967—the year that tensions erupted into warfare between Israel and her neighbors in the Arab world, resulting in the Israeli army occupation of the Palestinian-inhabited lands of the West Bank and Gaza. For the next twenty-three years Langer provided legal counsel to Palestinians whose human rights had been violated by the Israeli army and legal system. Because of Langer's political stance, her fellow Israelis ostracized and even threatened to kill her.

Flees from Nazi forces

Felicia Weid was born in Poland in 1930 to Jewish parents. At the outbreak of World War II (1939–45), Langer and her parents fled to Russia to escape Nazi persecution. (The Nazis—short for the National Socialist German Worker's Party—were an authoritarian and anti-Semitic political and military force headed by Adolf Hitler.) Langer's father died of starvation along the way.

After the war Langer found that all her relatives had perished in the Nazi death camps. She returned to Poland, and her mother moved to Israel. Langer married Moshe Langer, a survivor of five Nazi death camps, and in 1950 the couple moved to Israel to be near Langer's mother.

Langer became an Israeli citizen and studied to become a lawyer. In 1965 she went to work for a law firm in Tel Aviv. Langer and her husband, dismayed by what they came to believe was racism and economic inequality in Israeli society, joined the Israeli Communist Party. (Communism is the theory of social organization based on the holding of all property in common.)

Visits Palestinian towns after occupation

In the wake of the Six-Day War of June 1967 (see box), the Israeli army occupied the Palestinian-inhabited territories of the West Bank and Gaza. When Langer surveyed the ruins of three Palestinian villages—Ualu, Beit Nouba, and Amousas—that had been razed by the Israeli army, she became convinced that Palestinian lives were being destroyed and that they needed someone to defend them.

Langer learned of other actions of the occupation army, including the bulldozing of individual Palestinian homes, the confiscation of Palestinian lands, the jailings without charge of Palestinian youths, and the torture and killings of Palestinian activists. Langer pledged to devote her energies to helping Palestinians achieve justice. She quit her law job in Tel Aviv and opened a private practice in Jerusalem. She also began publishing articles in the Israeli press, denouncing the occupation.

Represents Palestinians in occupied territories

In the winter of 1967 Langer received her first Palestinian clients: a Muslim priest (called an imam) and his wife, whose son was in jail on charges of "membership in a Palestinian resistance organization." Over the next twenty-three years Langer represented thousands of Palestinians charged with political crimes. She sought relief for Arabs facing deportation or the demolition of their homes, those who had been brutalized by the Israeli military, and those jailed for political

A Short History of Israel and Palestine

The state of Israel was established in the Middle East in 1948, on land primarily inhabited by Arabs but with a significant population of Jewish refugees from Europe. The Arabs displaced by the new country, who began referring to themselves as Palestinians, were moved to refugee camps in the West Bank (of Jordan) and Gaza (of Egypt). As the years passed, resentment grew among the thousands of people whose refugee status seemed to have become permanent. In 1964 the Palestinian Liberation Organization (PLO) was formed as a guerrilla force dedicated to the overthrow of Israel. (In 1988 the PLO acknowledged Israel's right to exist and underwent a transformation from a military force to a political organization.)

A significant event in Israeli/Palestinian history was the Six-Day War in June 1967. Egypt moved troops into the Sinai, ordered the withdrawal of United Nations Emergency Forces, and closed the Strait of Tiran to Israeli shipping. The Israeli army retaliated and conquered the Jordanian lands of East Jerusalem and the West Bank, the Golan Heights of Syria, and the Sinai Desert (including Gaza) of Egypt. Israel annexed (made part of its territory) East Jerusalem (and in 1980 made the united city of Jerusalem its capital, though that is not recognized by the United Nations) and began a military occupation of the West Bank and Gaza. The Israeli military carried out many acts against Palestinian civilians—including beatings, torture, and jailings—that drew international criticism.

In the 1978 Camp David Accords (reached at Camp David, Maryland, with the participation of U.S. President Jimmy Carter), Israel promised to return the Sinai to Egypt. The agreement was widely opposed by other Arab countries, however, because it allowed Israel to maintain its occupation of the West Bank and Gaza. Also during that period Israel annexed the Golan Heights and tightened its control over the West Bank by expelling elected Arab mayors in many of the region's villages.

The year 1987 saw the start of the Palestinian Intifada (uprising) after twenty years of Israeli military occupation, which

offenses. Langer also fought for the right of Palestinian universities, newspapers, and economic institutions to stay open.

Langer appeared before the Israeli Supreme Court several times to argue the illegality of house demolitions, beatings, the use of plastic bullets against civilians, and other abuses that were in violation of the Geneva Convention (international human rights treaty adopted in 1926, to which Israel was a sig-

had brought unemployment, poverty, and repression. They boycotted Israeli goods, launched physical attacks (typically stone-throwing by masked youths) against Israeli troops, and held demonstrations for Palestinian statehood. The Israeli government responded with a fierce military crackdown and a suspension of civil liberties in the occupied territories. Human rights groups around the world, and even many Israeli citizens, condemned Israel's tactics.

A new round of Israeli-Palestinian peace talks began in 1993. The resulting Declaration of Principles on Interim Self-Government Arrangements, also known as the Oslo Accords, set out a time line for gradual Palestinian self-rule. The Palestinian Authority was created to govern Palestinian affairs, with PLO Chairman Yasser Arafat at the helm. As of May 1994, Israel had turned over 60 percent of the Gaza Strip and 3 percent of the West Bank to the Palestinian Authority.

By 1997, although Israeli troops had pulled out of seven major West Bank towns, far less land had been turned over to the Palestinian Authority than had been promised under the Oslo Accords. And Israel continued to build new settlements on occupied Palestinian lands, which caused growing frustration among Palestinians.

In the late 1990s terrorist attacks against Israeli civilians by the Islamic fundamentalist group Hamas became more frequent. In response to Hamas attacks, the Israeli government sealed off the occupied territories (preventing Palestinians from reaching their jobs in Israel) and withheld funding for municipal services. Since that time, little progress has been made in resolving the conflict. Meetings in July 2000, hosted by U.S. President Bill Clinton, between Israeli prime minister Ehud Barak and Palestinian authority president Yasser Arafat, were unsuccessful. Nevertheless, the dialogue remains open on the status of Jerusalem despite the deep historical and religious ties of the parties to the ancient city.

natory). Langer lost in virtually every case. In a series of rulings, the Israeli Supreme Court upheld the military's actions on political grounds.

Throughout her legal career, Langer saw few victories. Her greatest legal triumph, which came in 1979, was marred by tragedy. In that case Langer won the reinstatement of Bassam Shaka, the celebrated Arab mayor of Nablus, who had been expelled from the West Bank by the Israeli military governor. When the Supreme Court ruling came in Shaka's favor, all of Nablus celebrated. It was a hollow victory, though, because shortly afterwards Shaka lost his legs, and nearly lost his life, when a bomb exploded in his car.

Langer kept careful notes about her cases and wrote at length about human rights violations in Palestine. While in Israel, Langer wrote several books: *With My Own Eyes* (1975), *Those Are My Brothers* (1979), and *An Age of Stone* (1988). After moving to Germany in 1990 she authored three additional books about human rights abuses in the occupied territories: *Where Hatred Knows No Limits, Let Us Live as Human Beings,* and *Bridge of Dreams,* and a telephone-book sized autobiography titled *Fury and Hope.*

Harassed by her fellow Israelis

When Langer began representing Palestinians, her fellow Israelis began treating her as a traitor and an outcast. She endured death threats and physical assaults. A car tried to run her down on one occasion and on another, when she hurt her leg, she was refused treatment in a Jerusalem hospital. The pressure on Langer's only child, her son, became so intense that he decided to move out of the country.

Among Langer's most powerful enemies was the Jewish Defense League (JDL), a conservative Israeli paramilitary organization that commits acts of terrorism against Palestinians and their defenders. In 1984 members of the JDL spray-painted on Langer's door: "Felicia Langer is a PLO whore. The day of your death is near." (PLO stands for Palestinian Liberation Organization; see box on History of Israel and Palestine.)

Quits law practice and leaves Israel

Throughout her years defending Palestinians, Langer was treated with disdain by the Israeli military courts. Authorities often prevented Langer from meeting with her clients, they dismissed her petitions and scoffed at her appeals, and in many trials overruled her every argument. As inequitable as the military justice system was for the first twenty years of the occupation, in 1987—the year the Intifada (Palestinian uprising; see box on history of Israel and Palestine) began—it became even worse.

During the Intifada hundreds of Palestinians were rounded up daily and jailed. After spending months in overcrowded prisons or detention camps, they were herded through courtrooms in large groups. Each prisoner was expected to confess to political crimes or face a long sentence. "When the Intifada began, the situation became impossible," said Langer in a 1990 *Washington Post* interview. "The courts started to be overwhelmed by the massive arrests, and it started to resemble a factory, or a supermarket for setting punishment that only slightly resembled the administration of justice."

In 1990, thirty months after the start of the Intifada and twenty-three years after she began defending Palestinians, Langer decided to call it quits. "I realized that all this time, by bringing Palestinians to the courts, I had been legitimizing the system, but the system had not brought the Palestinians any justice," stated Langer in the *Washington Post* interview. She packed up her office and, with her husband, moved to Tubingen, Germany.

Continues writing and advocating on behalf of Palestinians

In Tubingen Langer received a university appointment to lecture about international law and the Israeli system of justice in the occupied territories. "The judicial system in Israel has to be exposed and condemned to death," declared Langer in a 1991 interview in *The Independent* of London, "and I could not do it while I was operating as a lawyer." In 1990, on her sixtieth birthday, Langer received the Right Livelihood Award (considered the alternative Nobel Peace Prize) in Stockholm, Sweden, "for the exemplary courage of her struggle for the basic rights of the Palestinian people."

In a 1998 interview in the Cairo (Egypt)-based *Al-Ahram Weekly*, Langer asserted that the situation for Palestinians in the occupied territories remained dire. From 1993 to 1998, she stated, "Israeli forces have killed and injured hundreds of Palestinians, destroyed the homes of over five hundred families, taken away the rights of over one thousand peo-

Palestinian Human Rights Lawyer Raji Sourani

Raji Sourani (1954-) is widely regarded as the foremost human rights attorney in Gaza. He is the director of the Palestinian Center for Human Rights—an agency that monitors and documents human rights violations committed by Israeli military forces and promotes democracy in Gaza.

Sourani rose to prominence during the 1980s for defending Palestinians being tried in Israeli military courts. Since 1987 (the year in which the Palestinian Intifada, or uprising, began) Israeli military authorities have retaliated against Sourani by jailing him six times (once for illegal political activity and the other times without charge) and subjecting him to beatings and other forms of physical abuse.

"We litigate cases with the prior knowledge that most of our cases will not obtain a fair hearing," stated Sourani in a 1991 *Boston Globe* interview. "The most we expect to achieve is some damage control, but we expect no victories. We lose more than 95 percent of our cases." In 1991 Sourani was awarded the Robert F. Kennedy Human Rights Award—a prize established in honor of slain U.S. Attorney General and presidential candidate Robert F. Kennedy (1925–1968).

In 1995 Sourani was twice detained by officers of the Palestinian Authority (the Palestinian self-rule governmental body established in May 1994 to run affairs in portions of Gaza and the West Bank). Sourani's "crime" was

ple to live in Jerusalem, arrested, imprisoned and tortured thousands of people, leaving other thousands homeless."

Sources

Books

Emerson, Gloria. *Gaza: A Year in the Intifada: A Personal Account from an Occupied Land.* New York: Atlantic Monthly Press, 1991.

Hass, Amira. *Drinking the Sea at Gaza: Days and Nights in a Land Under Siege.* Translated by Elana Wesley and Maxine Kaufman-Lacusta. New York: Metropolitan Books, 1996.

Langer, Felicia. *An Age of Stone.* Translated by Isaac Cohen. London, England: Quartet Books, 1988.

Wallach, John, and Janet Wallach. *The New Palestinians: The Emerging Generation of Leaders.* Rocklin, CA: Prima Publishing, 1992.

Raji Sourani. *Reproduced by permission of the Palestinian Center for Human Rights.*

publicly criticizing Palestinian Authority head Yasser Arafat's creation of military courts. In a letter released to the press, Sourani characterized the courts as a "drift away from democracy and governmental accountability, the stripping of the judiciary's independence and the removal of legal protection for the Palestinian people."

Also in 1995 Sourani's Palestinian Center for Human Rights was granted France's Human Rights Award—the most prestigious award given by France for human rights endeavors. As the new millennium began, Sourani was still defending torture victims and speaking out against abuses by both the Israeli military and the Palestinian Authority.

Articles

Di Giovanni, Janine. "The Israeli Who Stands Up for Palestinians." *The Independent (London)*. January 24, 1991: 16.

Diehl, Jackson. "Israeli Defender of Arab Rights Quits in 'Despair and Disgust.'" *Washington Post*. May 13, 1990: A23.

Farrell, John Aloysius. "Israeli, Arab get RFK Prize for Rights." *Boston Globe*. November 21, 1991: 22.

"Palestinian Rights Activist Warns of 'Extremely Bloody' Uprising." *Deutsche Press-Agentur*. June 9, 1998.

Web Sites

"1991 RFK Human Rights Award." Robert F. Kennedy Memorial. [Online] Available http://www.rfkmemorial.org/human_rights/1991.htm (accessed March 9, 2000).

"Felicia Langer (1990)." *The Right Livelihood Award.* [Online] Available http://www.rightlivelihood.se/recip1900_3.html (accessed March 9, 2000).

"Palestinian Centre for Human Rights Wins France's Highest Award for Human Rights Endeavours." Palestinian Centre for Human Rights (Press release, December 7, 1996). [Online] Available http://www.pchrgaza.com/files/PressR.html (accessed March 9, 2000).

Rady, Faiza. "A Portrait of Felicia Langer." *Al-Ahram Weekly.* [Online] Available http://www.ahram.org.eg/weekly/1998/1948/402_flci.htm (accessed March 13, 2000).

Rosa Luxemburg

Born March 5, 1871
Zamosc, Poland
Died January 15, 1919
Berlin, Germany

Revolutionary political leader, writer, and orator

Rosa Luxemburg was born at a time when monarchs ruled in Russia and Europe, and the majority of people lived in poverty. It was also a time of a growing movement of resistance to those rulers. Opposition activists generally embraced some form of socialism. Under a socialist system, power and resources would be wrested from the control of the ruler and the wealthy individuals who supported the ruler, and placed in the hands of the community as a whole.

Luxemburg became involved with socialist causes while a student and later established herself as a leading voice among turn-of-the-century European radicals. Her opposition to nationalism (pride in, and allegiance to, one's nation) and authoritarianism (the control of the will of the people by a leader or a group of leaders) put her at odds with other socialist leaders. Luxemburg envisioned an international socialist society, created by a massive workers' strike (work stoppage). She died fighting for her ideals. Luxemburg is remembered for her intelligence and her unwavering commitment to international socialism.

"Freedom only for the supporters of the government, only for the members of one Party, no matter how numerous they may be, is no freedom at all. Freedom is always and exclusively freedom for the one who thinks differently."

Rosa Luxemburg as quoted in The Nation

Rosa Luxemburg.
Courtesy of the Library of Congress.

Childhood in Poland

Rosa Luxemburg was born on March 5 of 1870 or 1871 (historians are divided as to the correct year) to a middle-class family of merchants. She was the youngest of five children. Luxemburg's home town of Zamosc, at the time of her birth, was part of the Russian empire. It had previously been part of the Independent Kingdom of Poland. Luxemburg's parents were of Jewish-German heritage.

Luxemburg's parents introduced her to classic European and Russian literature and instilled in her an appreciation for the arts and music. When Luxemburg was a child her family moved to Warsaw—also within the Russian empire. Luxemburg suffered a misdiagnosed illness as a child that left her with a permanent limp.

Continues education in Switzerland

Luxemburg was a brilliant student in high school; she loved learning and was not afraid to ask difficult questions. Also during high school Luxemburg participated in protests against the czar's (also spelled tsar; emperor of Russia) authoritarian rule. In 1886 she graduated at the top of her class. She then intensified her political activities and three years later was forced to flee the country to avoid arrest by the Russian secret police. Luxemburg moved to Zurich, Switzerland, and enrolled in the University of Zurich to study economics, philosophy, and law.

Zurich in the late 1800s was an international center of socialist activity. Exiled government critics from Russia, Germany, and other nations were granted asylum in neutral Switzerland. Luxemburg became close associates with a number of prominent socialists, including Russian revolutionaries Vladimir Lenin (1870–1924) and Georgi Plekhanov (1857–1918), German feminist and communist Clara Zetkin (1857–1933), and Polish activist Leo Jogiches. (Communism is a theory of social organization based on the holding of all property in common, overseen by a centralized government.) With Jogiches, Luxemburg had a brief romance and a lifelong working relationship.

While working toward a doctoral degree in economics, Luxemburg carefully studied the writings of the German economist and father of communist theory, **Karl Marx**

(1818–1883; see entry). Her evenings were occupied by long, passionate debates with her socialist colleagues about what form a socialist revolutionary society should take. Luxemburg completed and published a highly acclaimed dissertation on Poland's economic dependency on Russia. Her dissertation was later used by Poland's Social Democratic Party as a blueprint for the country's industrial development.

Rises in ranks of socialists in Germany

After completing her degree, Luxemburg moved to Berlin, Germany—the site of the largest and most vibrant socialist movement in Europe. She also chose Berlin because Marx had predicted in his writings that Germany, being the most highly industrialized nation in Europe, would experience the first workers' revolution.

As a Russian citizen, Luxemburg was not allowed to establish residency in Germany. She thus entered into a marriage of convenience with a German named Gustav Lubeck. Once she had settled in Berlin and attained German citizenship, she divorced Lubeck. Luxemburg made Berlin her home from 1899 until her death twenty years later, despite her distaste for the city. She characterized Berlin as the "most repulsive place: cold, ugly, massive, a real barracks."

Luxemburg became recognized as one of the foremost socialist thinkers in Germany, as well as the most powerful speaker on behalf of Germany's working class. She joined in the debate raging through the German socialist party at the turn of the century between those who believed in working for social change, one step at a time, through existing government structures, and those who believed in fostering a workers' revolution to create a society without social classes. Luxemburg was firmly in the latter camp, claiming that it was impossible to bring about socialism without a social revolution.

Activism, teaching, and writing

In 1905 Luxemburg traveled to Warsaw, where a workers' revolt against factory owners and landowners was underway. Soon after her arrival Luxemburg was arrested for her part in the uprising. She spent a few months in jail, during which time she became ill, and returned to Berlin upon her release.

Luxemburg and Lenin

Luxemburg enjoyed a long and close association with Russian revolutionary leader Vladimir Lenin (1870–1924). Their relationship began in 1890, when both were members of the exile community in Zurich, Switzerland. Luxemburg was not afraid to challenge Lenin—who was noted for his intolerance of opposition—regarding specific aspects of socialism on which they disagreed. Lenin respected Luxemburg for her sharp intellect, calling her an "eagle."

One point of contention between the two was the issue of nationalism. Luxemburg argued that patriotic allegiances distracted members of the working class from the ultimate goal of establishing a classless society (a society in which there would be no rich and poor, but in which everyone would be regarded as equals). Luxemburg viewed the struggle for socialism as an international one. Lenin, on the other hand, viewed nationalism as an expression of respect for national cultures. He argued that there was no contradiction between nationalism and socialism and that feelings of national pride could even be helpful in fostering socialist revolutions.

Another area of disagreement between Luxemburg and Lenin concerned the role of revolutionary leaders.

Vladimir Lenin. *Reproduced by permission of Archive Photos.*

Luxemburg was of the firm belief that revolutionary leaders should educate and empower the masses of workers to direct their own destiny. She favored the use of huge strikes and economic boycotts (refusal to buy certain products) to bring about revolutions, and mass participation in revolutionary governments. Lenin, in contrast, advocated that a revolution should be directed and controlled by a professional core of party activists. Luxemburg publicly criticized Lenin for being an authoritarian and cruel leader after Lenin's forces took power in Russia in 1917.

From 1907 to 1914 Luxemburg taught Marxist philosophy at a socialist school in Berlin and wrote several articles and books. Her best-known work of the period was *The Accumulation of Capital,* published in 1913. In that book she agreed with Marx's premise that capitalism would destroy itself, and theorized that the cause of capitalism's downfall would be factory owners fighting among themselves for control of labor and resources in poor nations.

Imprisoned for opposition to World War I

In 1914, when World War I (1914–18) broke out in Europe, German socialists were faced with the choice of whether or not to support their country in the war effort. While most of Luxemburg's colleagues stood with the German government, and even went off to fight and to die, Luxemburg stood firm in her opposition. She decried nationalism as being at odds with socialism, in that socialism required international solidarity. In other words, Luxemburg believed that the allegiance of workers of different nations should be to one another, and not to their respective governments.

Luxemburg was outspoken in her opposition to the war and to socialist participation in it. Her leadership of the antiwar movement landed her in jail in 1915. Except for one brief period of freedom, Luxemburg was incarcerated until the war's end in 1918. She passed her time behind bars reading books on politics, art, and music, and writing lengthy letters to her friends who also opposed the war.

In 1917, during a brief release from jail, Luxemburg formed an organization with other anti-World War I socialists that aimed to end the war by encouraging revolution in Germany. They called the organization the Spartacus League, after the Greek slave Spartacus who led a rebellion against the Romans in the first century B.C. The Spartacus League, however, gained few converts. It was no match for the patriotism and fervid support of war that had swept the continent.

Killed during communist rebellion in Germany

Luxemburg was released from prison in November 1918, when Germany was defeated in the war and Kaiser Wilhelm II (1859–1941; last German kaiser 1888–1918) fled the country. A group of moderate socialists formed a new government and, being careful to keep the military on their side, began to rebuild the nation. Luxemburg criticized government leaders for not turning control of resources over to the workers and for not taking other steps to create a socialist republic. In December 1918 she and a cofounder of the Spartacus League, Karl Liebknecht, formed a new party, the Communist Party of Germany, to challenge the socialists in power.

Luxemburg and her Communist Party colleagues immediately began organizing a massive work stoppage that they believed would bring down the government. They had considerable success in organizing workers in Berlin, and by January 1919 Berlin was in a state of civil war.

The armed forces moved in swiftly and brutally to crush the rebellion. On January 15, just six days into the battle, Luxemburg and Liebknecht were captured by the army. Luxemburg was shot in a military vehicle and her body was thrown into the Landwehr canal in downtown Berlin. The men who killed her later became officers in Hitler's Nazi army. Luxemburg continues to be revered as a hero and a martyr by European socialists.

Sources

Books

Basso, Lelio. *Rosa Luxemburg: A Reappraisal*. Translated by Douglas Parmée. New York: Praeger, 1967.

Bronner, Stephen Eric, ed. *The Letters of Rosa Luxemburg*. Boulder, CO: Westview Press, 1978.

Ettinger, Elzbieta. *Rosa Luxemburg: A Life*. Boston: Beacon Press, 1986.

"Rosa Luxemburg." In *Historic World Leaders*. Detroit: Gale Research, 1994.

Articles

Egger, Daniel. "Rosa Luxemburg." *The Nation*. April 25, 1987: 546+. (Movie.)

Egger, Daniel. Review of *Rosa Luxemburg: A Life. The Nation*. April 25, 1987: 546+.

Samora Machel

Born September 29, 1933
Chilembene, Mozambique
Died October 19, 1986
Mbuzini, Lemombo Mountains, South Africa

**Independence leader and first
president of Mozambique**

Samora Machel, who became president of Mozambique in 1975, attempted to raise the country's standard of living by nationalizing (putting into government ownership) industries and land, and providing free education and health care. His program never had a chance to succeed, however, as the nation came under attack by a South African-backed, counterrevolutionary armed force. Machel died in a plane crash near the South African border in 1986; many people continue to suspect the South African government of sabotage in the incident.

Reared in region with history of rebellion

Samora Machel (pronounced ma-SHELL) was born in 1933 in the Mozambican village of Chilembene. That village, in the Gaza Province, was the site of an armed uprising against the Portuguese army in the 1890s. Although the army had crushed the force of local warriors, the spirit of resistance in the province had survived.

Machel's parents were highly respected community leaders and farmers. They achieved a measure of success with

"We do not recognize tribes, regions, race, or religious belief. We only recognize Mozambicans who are equally exploited and equally desirous of freedom and revolution."

Samora Machel, Mozambique Independence Day speech given in 1975.

Samora Machel.
Reproduced by permission of Archive Photos.

their farming operation despite the oppressive rules of the colonial government. (Colonialism is the policy by which one nation exerts control over another nation or territory.) Machel's parents, being native African farmers, received lower prices for their crops than did white farmers. They were also forced to grow cotton—a cash crop from which the colonial power profited handsomely—instead of growing food crops for their own subsistence (to sustain their lives). Nevertheless, through hard work they managed to accumulate several plows and four hundred head of cattle.

Education directed by missionaries

Machel, at the age of nine, was sent by his parents to a school run by Catholic missionaries (missionaries were the sole providers of education for black children in the nation) in the town of Souguene. There he received religious education as well as lessons in Portuguese language and culture. Machel allowed himself to be baptized—a requirement for attending high school—only to find out that after high school he would be compelled to enter the priesthood. Machel opted, instead, to enroll in nursing school in the capital city of Lourenço Marques (now Maputo).

Joins movement against colonialism

After completing his training in nursing, Machel found employment at the Miguel Bombarda Hospital. There he was dismayed at the disparity in the quality of medical care given to white colonialists (who were generally wealthy) and black native Mozambicans (who were generally poor). Machel noted that health care was just one of many areas in which blacks were discriminated against by the colonial authorities.

In 1961 Machel joined an anticolonial student group called the Nucleus of Mozambican Students (NESAM). NESAM had been formed by Eduardo Mondlane, a Mozambican sociologist who had been educated in the United States at Northwestern University in Evanston, illinois. As Machel's involvement with NESAM grew, his activities came to the attention of the colonial government's secret police.

In 1963, upon learning he was soon to be arrested, Machel fled the country. He headed for Tanzania (the nation bordering Mozambique to the north), where Mondlane had established an armed resistance movement to the Portuguese colonial army called the Front for the Liberation of Mozambique (FRELIMO). Machel was sent to Algeria for a year of military training, after which he returned to Tanzania.

Rises in ranks of FRELIMO

Machel's tactical skills rapidly became apparent to the FRELIMO leadership. In 1964 he was assigned to head a training camp, where the recruits included young people from the countryside, educated urban youths, and a few deserters from the Portuguese army. That same year Machel began leading military raids into Mozambique. In 1966 he was appointed commander of FRELIMO's Defense Department and made a member of the policy-setting central committee. Machel was responsible for the development of social services—such as agricultural cooperatives, literacy classes, and low-cost stores—for FRELIMO members.

In 1970, after the assassination of Mondlane, Machel was made president of FRELIMO. That same year he married Josina Muthemba, a fellow freedom-fighter; he was greatly saddened by her death two years later. In 1975 Machel married Graca Simbine.

Ascends to presidency of Mozambique

Throughout the early 1970s, FRELIMO won a series of battles against the Portuguese forces. By 1974 the colonial government had collapsed and Portugal was ready to hold negotiations with FRELIMO. The talks led to Mozambique's independence on June 25, 1975. On that date, 470 years of Portuguese colonial rule ended and Machel became the new republic's first president.

"We do not recognize tribes, regions, race, or religious belief," stated Machel in his Independence Day speech. "We only recognize Mozambicans who are equally exploited and equally desirous of freedom and revolution."

Machel found himself at the helm of a nation beset by 90 percent illiteracy, rampant medical problems, and poverty. In an attempt to remedy these problems, he announced a socialist program based on the teachings of German economic

Congolese Independence Leader Patrice Lumumba

Patrice Lumumba (1925–1961) was an anticolonial leader who became the first prime minister of independent Congo (renamed Zaire upon independence). Lumumba was educated at schools run by Catholic and Protestant missionaries. As a young adult, while working as a post office clerk, he expanded his breadth of knowledge by reading books sent to him by professors in Europe. The more he learned, the deeper his commitment ran to opposing the Belgian colonial government.

In 1958 Lumumba founded the Congolese National Movement (MNC), which advocated immediate and total independence. He attended the first All-African People's Conference in Ghana (one of the first African nations to achieve independence), after which he was briefly jailed for political agitation. Upon his release, Lumumba traveled to Belgium to discuss the future government structure of the Congo.

On June 30, 1960, the Congo was granted independence. Lumumba was elected prime minister of the new state, called Zaire, by a sweeping majority.

Patrice Lumumba. *Reproduced by permission of AP/Wide World Photos.*

Almost as soon as Lumumba took office he faced military unrest, which had been fostered by Belgium and the United States (those two nations had benefitted from the exploitation of the Congo's vast natural resources during the colonial era). Lumumba was arrested in January 1961 and killed while in the custody of military officers and Belgian mercenaries.

theorist **Karl Marx** (1818–1883; see entry). (Socialism is a type of social and economic organization based on the control of the means of production by the community as a whole, rather than by wealthy individuals or corporations.)

Specifically, Machel placed abandoned businesses and houses, as well as large tracts of land and important industries, under government control. He set up free schools and health clinics throughout the nation, and made available free legal services. Machel stressed gender and racial equality and appointed numerous women and people of all races to key government posts. He also tried to rid the country of rivalries based on tribal affiliation.

Faces economic crisis, raids by guerrilla forces

It is not known whether Machel's prescription would have cured his nation's ills, for almost immediately the nation came under economic and military attack. Some two hundred thousand Portuguese citizens evacuated the nation—taking with them a large portion of Mozambique's capital. Many destroyed property, equipment, and cattle as they left. In 1976 Rhodesia, which had previously been one of Mozambique's main trading partners, further crippled the economy by cutting off commerce with Mozambique. (Rhodesia was a British colony until 1980, when the black majority took over and renamed it Zimbabwe.)

Rhodesia's white prime minister Ian Smith upped the destabilization effort by sponsoring a guerrilla force, called the Mozambique National Resistance (RENAMO), aimed at toppling Machel's government. Upon Smith's decline from power in 1980, South Africa (which was under white minority rule until 1990) took over support of RENAMO, providing training bases, arms and supplies (which they airlifted to RENAMO forces inside Mozambique), and logistical support.

RENAMO forces throughout the 1980s killed hundreds of thousands of Mozambicans in gruesome manners and made some three million homeless. Their widespread use of land mines—and the civilian loss of limbs that resulted—drew international condemnation. RENAMO destroyed countless acres of crops, some 1,800 schools, more than seven hundred health centers, nine hundred shops, and more than one thousand vehicles.

Negotiates nonaggression pact with South Africa

Mozambique's economy was in shambles in the early 1980s, due to the effects of a drought and famine, inefficiency of government-controlled industries, and the need to spend 42 percent of the nation's budget defending the populace from RENAMO. In 1984 Machel negotiated a truce with the South African government, called the Nkomati Accord, under which he agreed to expel the military wing of the African National Congress (the organization trying to overthrow the white-minority government in South Africa) from Mozambique in exchange for the South African government's discontinuance of aid to RENAMO.

Machel upheld his end of the bargain, but South African President P. W. Botha did not. RENAMO raids from South Africa continued, and the South African government continued to supply RENAMO with covert (secret) assistance. Although RENAMO's terrorist tactics were denounced by the international community, the force was not disbanded until 1992.

Dies in plane crash

Machel died in a plane crash in the Lemombo Mountains along South Africa's northern border on October 19, 1986. He had been returning from a conference of the frontline black African nations (the nations bordering South Africa) in Zambia.

Many people suspected South African officials of somehow having caused the crash. There was speculation that the plane's instrument panel had been tampered with and that radio signals had been scrambled in an attempt to make the pilot misjudge his location. Those accusations had been fueled, in part, by a statement made by South Africa's Defense Minister Magnus Malan just ten days before the crash. Malan had blamed Machel for the October 6 deaths of six South African soldiers who had stepped on a land mine, near the borders of South Africa, Mozambique, and Swaziland (very close to the site of the plane crash.) "Terror feeds on itself," Malan had stated. "It eventually turns on its hosts."

Sources

Books

Carter, Gwendolen M., and Patrick O'Meara, eds. *African Independence: The First Twenty-Five Years*. Bloomington: Indiana University Press, 1985.

Finnegan, William. *A Complicated War: The Harrowing of Mozambique.* Berkeley: University of California Press, 1992.

"Machel, Samora Moises." *Current Biography Yearbook 1984.* Edited by Charles Moritz. New York: H. W. Wilson Company, 1984, pp. 248–51.

Middleton, John, ed. *Encyclopedia of Africa South of the Sahara.* Vol. 3. New York: Charles Scribner's Sons, 1997, pp. 61–62, 71–72, 191–198.

Articles

Askin, Steve, and Colin Darch. "Southern Africa—Hope Deferred." *The Nation.* May 28, 1990: 725+.

"Mozambique Remembers Samora Machel." *Electronic Mail and Guardian.* (Johannesburg, South Africa). October 20, 1998.

Serrill, Michael S. "Anger over a Plane Crash; A Leader's Death Adds More Instability to a Country on Its Knees." *Time.* November 3, 1986: 40.

Malcolm X

Born May 19, 1925
Omaha, Nebraska
Died February 21, 1965
Harlem, New York

**African American advocate for black nationalism
and Nation of Islam minister and spokesman**

"If they make the Ku Klux Klan nonviolent, I'll be nonviolent. If they make the White Citizen's Council nonviolent, I'll be nonviolent."

Malcolm X in a speech in 1965.

Malcolm X.
Reproduced by permission of AP/Wide World Photos.

The life of Malcolm X was a complex journey from rural schoolboy, to convicted felon, to Muslim preacher, to militant political leader. With his gift for fiery oration, Malcolm X inspired African Americans throughout the nation to fight for their rights. He rejected the civil rights movement's premises of nonviolence and integration and instead stressed the need for African Americans to defend themselves and form their own institutions.

Until the final year of his life, Malcolm X spread the Nation of Islam's message of hatred toward white America and pride in black America. After a pilgrimage through the Middle East in 1964, however, Malcolm X renounced racial animosity. He ended his association with the Nation of Islam and formed his own black nationalist organization, the Organization of Afro-American Unity.

Malcolm X was gunned down while delivering a speech in 1965. Even in death, however, he continues to inspire activists in the struggle for African American rights.

Early exposure to violence

Malcolm X was born Malcolm Little in Nebraska in 1925. His father, a Baptist preacher named Earl Little, was a follower of Marcus Garvey (1887–1940; Jamaican black nationalist leader who advocated that all black people return to Africa). When Malcolm was four years old, his home was set on fire by Ku Klux Klan members. (The Ku Klux Klan is a white supremacist organization known for its intimidation and acts of violence against African Americans and members of other racial, ethnic, and religious minorities.) After that attack, the Little family moved to Milwaukee, Wisconsin, and then to Lansing, Michigan. Shortly thereafter, when Malcolm was six years old, his father was killed. The suspects were members of a white supremacist group called the Black Legion.

A difficult youth

Malcolm's mother, living in poverty and suffering from a mental breakdown, was unable to support her eight children. The children were sent to foster homes around the state. Malcolm was sent to East Lansing. An excellent student and class leader, Malcolm aspired to be a doctor or a lawyer. His hopes were dashed, however, when a teacher told him it was not realistic for an African American to wish to become a professional. Malcolm lost interest in school and dropped out in the eighth grade.

At the age of fifteen, Malcolm moved to Boston, Massachusetts, to live with his half-sister, Ella. Malcolm found a job shining shoes and learned about life on the city streets, including drugs, gambling, and crime. Three years later Malcolm moved to Harlem, New York, where he earned his money selling marijuana and cocaine, running a gambling game called "the numbers," and luring customers into houses of prostitution. He then moved back to Boston and got involved in a burglary ring. At the age of twenty-one, Malcolm was convicted on burglary charges and sentenced to eight to ten years in prison.

Introduction to Nation of Islam

While in prison, Malcolm learned about the Nation of Islam (NOI) and its black Muslim leader, Elijah Muhammad (1897–1975). Malcolm was attracted to the NOI's strict regi-

Malcolm X addressing a rally in 1963.
Reproduced by permission of UPI/Corbis-Bettmann.

ment of prayer and self-discipline and its message that blacks were superior to whites. The NOI asserted that African Americans could only reclaim their rightful heritage by converting to Islam—their true religion. For Malcolm, whose family had been destroyed and whose aspirations had been dashed by whites, the teachings of the NOI helped him understand those events and gave him an outlet for his anger.

Along with Malcolm's conversion to Islam came a desire for learning and self-improvement. He read every book he could find in prison and even copied by hand a dictionary to improve his penmanship. In adherence to his Muslim faith, Malcolm stopped smoking, drinking, and eating pork and kept himself immaculately groomed. He also preached the teachings of Elijah Muhammad to other prisoners.

Rises to prominence in Nation of Islam

Upon his release from prison in 1952, Malcolm replaced his surname "Little" with "X." He took this step to rid

Activists, Rebels, and Reformers

himself of the name given to his great-grandparents, who were slaves, by their owners. "X" was the Muslim designation for the unknown surname of a black American's African ancestors.

Malcolm moved to Harlem and began preaching the NOI's message on street corners. He was ordained a minister in the NOI by Elijah Muhammad and assigned his own mosque (Muslim place of worship), first in Detroit, Michigan, and then in Philadelphia, Pennsylvania. Soon thereafter Malcolm was chosen to head the mosque in Harlem, which he built into the largest in the nation.

From 1952 to 1963 Malcolm's effectiveness as a preacher earned him the position of national spokesperson for the NOI, making him second-in-command to Elijah Muhammad. He toured widely in the United States during that time, delivering lectures to huge crowds at universities, speaking on radio and television programs, and establishing dozens of mosques. During Malcolm's years as NOI spokesperson, membership in the organization grew from about four hundred to ten thousand people.

In 1958 Malcolm married Betty Shabazz, whom he met at the Brooklyn State Hospital where Shabazz was a nursing student. The couple eventually had six children, including twins born after their father's death. In 1964 Malcolm wrote to Alex Haley (author; 1921–1992), his biographer, "Without her [Betty's] high morale I could never take my place in history."

Disagrees with civil rights leaders

In the 1960s, when most civil rights leaders were striving for integration and nonviolence, Malcolm advocated separatism and self-defense. Malcolm believed in fighting back against racial violence and seizing self-determination "by any means necessary." He pushed for African Americans to create and control their own economy, institutions, and politics. Because of his beliefs, Malcolm was characterized as dangerous and evil by the media. While he was loved by his followers, he was feared by most whites and many blacks.

Malcolm did not believe that true integration, where African Americans and whites would come together as equals, was possible in a racist society. He argued that if African Americans were allowed to enter white institutions, they would be forced to assimilate (become like the whites). Furthermore, Malcolm believed that integration would only accommodate middle-class African Americans, at the exclusion of the African American underclass.

Malcolm was sharply critical of the civil rights movement's emphasis on nonviolence. "If they make the Ku Klux Klan nonviolent, I'll be nonviolent," he stated in a speech given January 1, 1965. "If they make the White Citizen's Council nonviolent, I'll be nonviolent. . . . If someone puts a hand on you, send him to the cemetery." [White Citizens Councils were groups of southern whites, mostly from middle and professional classes, who sought to forestall the economic and political advancement of African Americans.]

Suspended from the Nation of Islam

As Malcolm's popularity grew, so did tensions between himself and Elijah Muhammad. Muhammad felt his own position threatened by Malcolm's rising prominence. At the same time, Malcolm was critical of Muhammad's sexual indiscretions. The final straw came in November 1963, when Malcolm made a public statement that the assassination of President John F. Kennedy (1917–1963; president 1961–63) was a case of "chickens coming home to roost." Malcolm later explained that what he meant by the statement was that "the country's climate of hate had killed the president." Muhammad, who was perhaps looking for an excuse to dismiss Malcolm, claimed that Malcolm's statement about the revered American president had alienated too many NOI supporters. He suspended Malcolm from the NOI in December 1963.

Conducts prayer pilgrimage

In March 1964 Malcolm made a permanent break with the NOI. Later that spring he conducted a prayer pilgrimage to the Middle East and Africa. On that journey he met Muslims of all races, praying together and living together as equals. Malcolm realized that people need not be divided because of the color of their skin, which precipitated a fundamental shift in his thinking. He no longer accepted the NOI characterization of white people as "blue-eyed devils." He came to see economic inequality as the true reason for African Americans' oppression.

Yuri Kochiyama Shares Malcolm's Passion for Justice

One of Malcolm X's closest friends was a leading Asian American activist named Yuri Kochiyama (1922–). Kochiyama, who is of Japanese ancestry, spent more than four decades fighting for social and economic justice for all people of color. Overcoming racial and cultural barriers, Kochiyama worked with the **Black Panther Party** (mid-1960s black power organization; see entry), the Young Lords Party (militant Puerto Rican rights group), the Asian American rights movement, the anti-Vietnam War movement, Puerto Rican independence groups, the movement to support political prisoners, and the campaign for reparations for survivors of Japanese American internment camps (centers in the United States in which Japanese Americans were imprisoned during World War II [1939–45]).

Kochiyama and Malcolm first met in the summer of 1963 in a Brooklyn courthouse, following the arrest of Kochiyama and several other people who had been protesting unfair hiring practices at a construction site. Kochiyama was familiar with the separatist teachings of Malcolm, as well as the appeals for integration by other civil rights leaders. Prior to meeting Malcolm, Kochiyama had believed that it was sufficient to fight for people's basic needs—education, housing, health care, and jobs. Malcolm taught her that oppressed people must learn about their history in order to effect social change and achieve equality. Kochiyama became an adherent of Malcolm X and became active in his Organization of Afro-American Unity.

Kochiyama was present at Malcolm's final speech, in February 1965 at Harlem's Audubon Ballroom. Kochiyama heard gunshots ring out and saw Malcolm fall. "I just went straight to Malcolm and I put his head on my lap," stated Kochiyama in a *New York Times* article of September 22, 1996. "He just lay there. He had difficulty breathing and he didn't utter a word." Every year on May 19, Malcolm's birthday, Kochiyama joins others in a pilgrimage to his gravesite in upstate New York.

"Malcolm X was the one person who changed my life more than anyone else," said Kochiyama in the video documentary *Yuri Kochiyama: Passion for Justice*, "because he gave me a different perspective of the struggle in America."

"Since I learned the *truth* in Mecca," wrote Malcolm in his autobiography, "my dearest friends have come to include *all* kinds—some Christians, Jews, Buddhists, Hindus, agnostics, and even atheists! I have friends who are called capitalists, Socialists, and Communists! Some of my friends are moderates, conservatives, extremists—some are even Uncle Toms! My friends today are black, brown, red, yellow, and *white!*"

Forms Organization of Afro-American Unity

Malcolm's experiences in the holy land of Mecca, Saudi Arabia, led him to convert to orthodox Islam and change his name to El-Hajj Malik El-Shabazz. He returned to the United States to establish the Muslim Mosque of Harlem and a black-nationalist group, the Organization of Afro-American Unity (OAAU). The OAAU advocated that African Americans practice self-defense, study African history and reclaim African culture, aspire to economic self-sufficiency, and become active in their communities. The OAAU stressed black pride and supported human rights around the world. The organization also called upon the United Nations to conduct an investigation into racial injustices in the United States.

The death of Malcolm X

After Malcolm returned from his pilgrimage, hostilities increased between himself and the NOI. Malcolm's former colleagues in the NOI were disdainful of Malcolm and the OAAU and feared losing their base of support to Malcolm. For his part, Malcolm criticized Elijah Muhammad for having extramarital affairs and called him a "racist" and a "political fakir" (imposter).

After receiving a series of death threats, Malcolm's house was firebombed on February 14, 1965. One week later, as Malcolm spoke before a huge crowd in Harlem's Audubon Ballroom, he was shot to death. While three men with ties to the NOI were convicted of the murder, there is speculation that the Federal Bureau of Investigation (FBI) and other government agencies may have played a role in the assassination plot.

Shortly after Malcolm's death, and largely due to his influence, the black power movement gained momentum. Favored by young and militant African Americans, black power was synonymous with racial pride. It represented the belief that blacks did not have to ask whites for acceptance, but that blacks held the power to create a better society for themselves. It represented the desire of African Americans to hold political, economic, and social power.

Sources

Books

Levy, Peter B. *The Civil Rights Movement.* Westwood, CT: Greenwood Press, 1998.

Malcolm X, and Alex Haley. *The Autobiography of Malcolm X.* New York: Grove Press, 1965.

Malcolm X Talks to Young People: Speeches in the U.S., Britain, and Africa. New York: Pathfinder Press, 1965.

O'Reilly, Kenneth. *Black Americans: The FBI Files.* New York: Carroll and Graf Publishers, Inc., 1994.

Smallwood, David, et. al. *Profiles of Great African Americans.* Lincolnwood, IL: Publications International, Ltd., 1996, pp. 208–11.

Articles

Onishi, Norimitsu. "Harlem's Japanese Sister." *The New York Times.* September 22, 1996: 41, 47.

Other Sources

Yuri Kochiyama: Passion for Justice. Produced and directed by Rea Tajiri and Pat Saunders. YK Project, 1993. Videocassette.

Nelson Mandela

Born July 18, 1918
Umtata, South Africa

**Political activist and former president
of South Africa**

"By transcending the horrors of his [Mandela's] time, he not only brought freedom to South Africa but also reflected the very best of the human spirit."

Donna E. Shalala, U.S. Secretary of Health and Human Services, upon nominating Mandela for Time *magazine's Person of the Century.*

Nelson Mandela.
Reproduced by permission of Reuters/Corbis-Bettmann

Nelson Mandela stands as an icon of courage, justice, and perseverance to people in South Africa and throughout the world. Imprisoned in 1964 for treason, stemming from his activities with the banned African National Congress (ANC), Mandela maintained his dignity behind bars and became an international symbol of human rights. Throughout the 1980s the rallying cry "Free Mandela" resounded on city streets and college campuses everywhere.

Mandela was freed in 1990, as a result of the tremendous economic and political pressure placed on the South African government by the international community. He resumed leadership of the ANC and, after a triumphant speaking and fund-raising tour across three continents, entered into talks with President F. W. deKlerk regarding the future of South Africa. The result was the dismantling of apartheid (the form of government based on racial segregation and discrimination) and the establishment of South Africa's first multiracial elections. In 1994 Mandela became the first president of a free South Africa. He retired from that position in 1999.

Groomed to be a tribal chief

Nelson Mandela was born into a highly respected family in the rural region of Umtata (later renamed the Transkei homeland—homelands were places into which blacks were forced to move). Mandela's father, Henry Mandela, was an advisor to the Tembu tribal chief. The family farmed and raised cattle. Henry died when Mandela was twelve years old, and Mandela was sent to live with the chief. Tribal members expected that Mandela would be their next chief.

As a teenager, Mandela decided to leave Umtata and become a lawyer. Mandela first attended Fort Hare College. After his expulsion from the college in 1940 for leading a student strike, Mandela completed his undergraduate training at Witwaterstrand University. Mandela then moved to an area outside of Johannesburg, South Africa, where he worked in the gold mines and took law classes by correspondence from the University of South Africa. Mandela received his law degree in 1942.

In 1944 Mandela married a nurse named Evelyn Ntoko Mase; the marriage ended in divorce in 1956. From that marriage Mandela had three children, one of whom died.

Joins the African National Congress

During the time that Mandela was a student, South Africa was governed by a system of racial segregation and discrimination called apartheid. Dismantled in the early 1990s, apartheid, which is an Afrikaaner (variation of Dutch spoke by white South Africans) word for "apartness," was a collection of more than six hundred laws governing every aspect of the lives of blacks, Indians, and mixed-race people. The white minority dictated to the black majority where they could live, work, and go to school. Nonwhites were not allowed to vote and had to carry identification papers with them at all times.

When he was twenty-four years old, Mandela joined the African National Congress (ANC)—a group that fought for political and economic rights for black South Africans. The ANC pursued legal and constitutional strategies, such as testifying before parliament and submitting petitions.

Mandela and several other ANC members organized a committee dedicated to nonviolent action in pursuit of the ANC's goals, called the Congress Youth League. The formation of the Youth League marked a radical departure from the ANC's traditional tactics in that the Youth League used direct action as a means of pressuring the government to change. The Youth League sponsored "stay at home days" during which black South Africans would not report for work or school, and held rallies to protest the unjust laws.

First arrest for antiapartheid activities

Police response to the Youth League's nonviolent activities grew increasingly brutal. From 1950 to 1952 several blacks were killed, beaten, and jailed during strikes and rallies. Mandela was among those arrested in 1952 for opposing the South African government. He was given a nine-month suspended sentence (meaning that he would not have to serve jail time) and was ordered to discontinue his involvement with the ANC.

After his trial Mandela quietly continued his political activism, organizing ANC members into a nationwide underground network. At the same time Mandela joined forces with another ANC leader, Oliver Tambo, to form the nation's first black law partnership.

Tried and acquitted of treason

In 1955, then a national organizer for the ANC, Mandela resumed publicly agitating for black freedom. The South African government had begun tightening restrictions on black organizations, and the police had intensified their attacks on apartheid opponents. In 1956 Mandela was arrested, along with 155 other antiapartheid leaders. He was charged with treason under the Suppression of Communism Act, even though he had never espoused communism (the theory of social organization based on the holding of all property in common).

Mandela was freed on bail and acted as his own defense during the very long "Treason Trial." He used the courtroom as a forum in which to advocate equal rights for South Africans of all races. At the same time Mandela kept working with the ANC, even though that activity was forbidden as a condition of his bail.

In 1958 Mandela married his second wife, a social worker and ANC activist named Winnie Madikizela (see box). Mandela and the other ANC leaders were acquitted of treason charges finally in 1961.

| **Activists, Rebels, and Reformers**

Sharpeville massacre marks turning point

In 1960, while Mandela's treason trial dragged on, an incident occurred that made many black opposition leaders—including Mandela—question the usefulness of nonviolent tactics. That incident was the Sharpeville massacre, in which police killed sixty-nine unarmed black protesters in the suburb of Sharpeville, outside of Johannesburg. Blacks throughout the nation were outraged by the killings. The government, anticipating unrest, banned the ANC and other antiapartheid organizations. Many black leaders, including Mandela, were rounded up and jailed.

Mandela expressed his willingness to confront violence with violence at a 1961 speech before the Pan-Africanist Conference in Ethiopia. (Pan-Africanism is the movement for a political alliance between all African nations.) "Peace in our country must be considered already broken," stated Mandela, "when a minority government maintains its authority over the majority by force and violence."

Mandela put his words into action by forming a group called Spear of the Nation, the purpose of which was to destroy property and equipment at government sites and at other institutions that supported apartheid. Mandela traveled throughout the country in secret, raising funds to support his mission. Within a year of its formation, Spear of the Nation had committed at least seventy acts of sabotage. The group continued operating as the military arm of the ANC until 1991.

Sentenced to life imprisonment for treason

Mandela was arrested in August 1962 and charged with organizing demonstrations on behalf of the banned ANC. Again Mandela acted as his own lawyer, basing his defense on the illegitimacy of the white-minority government. He was convicted and sentenced to five years in prison.

While Mandela was serving his sentence, police learned of Mandela's association with Spear of the Nation. Mandela was then charged with the more serious crimes of treason and sabotage. In June 1964 Mandela was convicted of those crimes and sentenced to life in prison.

Twenty-seven years as a prisoner

Mandela spent the first part of his life sentence at Robben Island prison, off South Africa's southwest coast. There he was made to do hard labor, such as mining limestone and harvesting seaweed. In an attempt to make the populace forget Mandela, the government had outlawed the mere mention of his name. Except for occasional visitors to the prison, Mandela was allowed no contact with the outside world. The government's strategy, however, backfired. It only served to elevate Mandela's stature in the eyes of black South Africans and the international community.

In 1982, when government officials became alarmed at Mandela's influence on other prisoners, they moved Mandela to a maximum-security facility called Pollsmoor Prison (outside of Cape Town, South Africa). For six years they held Mandela in solitary confinement. His long stretch of monotony was broken up only by weekly, thirty-minute visits from his wife.

In 1984 the government, facing increasing pressure from black South Africans and the outside world to free Mandela, offered his release if he would agree to settle in the black homeland of Transkei. Mandela rejected the offer and reaffirmed his allegiance to the ANC. The following year President P. W. Botha offered Mandela another deal: he would be released on the condition that he would renounce violence. Mandela stood firm, refusing to make such a statement until blacks were guaranteed full political rights.

South Africa feels the effect of international pressure

Throughout the 1980s, the international community stepped up pressure on the South African regime to end its policy of apartheid and to free political prisoners. The main tool used in the antiapartheid campaign was economic sanctions. Consumers pressured multinational corporations to pull out of South Africa. Businesses that remained in the country faced divestment of their stocks by state and local governments, universities, and other institutions. International human rights organizations regularly attacked South Africa for its abuses toward its black citizenry.

South Africa, which had become a pariah in the eyes of the world, faced political isolation and economic strangulation. As the year 1990 approached, it became clear that the country's survival depended upon the release of Mandela and other political prisoners, as well as the sharing of power with the black majority.

World welcomes Mandela's release from prison

In 1988 Mandela was hospitalized with tuberculosis—an infectious disease of the lungs. After his recovery, his imprisonment continued under much more humane conditions at Verster Prison. The South African government, by that time, recognized the enormous political cost of Mandela's incarceration. In his years behind bars, Mandela had become the world's most celebrated and respected political prisoner. He was a hero to black South African youth, who in the late 1980s had become increasingly brazen in their clashes with the police.

In 1989 the reins of the presidency were transferred to F. W. deKlerk, considered to be politically moderate. DeKlerk realized the futility of trying to hold onto white minority rule. As a peace gesture toward the black majority, deKlerk freed numerous imprisoned antiapartheid leaders and legalized the ANC and other banned organizations. Then, on February 11, 1990, he authorized Mandela's release. In an event broadcast to television audiences around the world, a gray-haired yet smiling and energetic Mandela exited the prison gates.

Mandela walked into a huge crowd of reporters, camera operators, and well-wishers. "When I was among the crowd I raised my right fist and there was a roar," Mandela wrote in his autobiography *Long Walk to Freedom*. "I had not been able to do that for twenty-seven years and it gave me a surge of strength and joy. . . . I felt—even at the age of seventy-one—that my life was beginning anew. My ten thousand days of imprisonment were over."

Negotiates multiracial government with deKlerk

Mandela immediately rejoined the leadership of the ANC and persuaded his comrades to suspend the armed struggle

Winnie Madikizela-Mandela

Winnie Madikizela was a social worker and ANC activist when she married Nelson Mandela in 1958. After giving birth to two daughters, Winnie Mandela realized that hers was not going to be a typical marriage. Nelson Mandela, an ANC leader conducting clandestine (secret) anti-government operations, told his wife that she would have to be strong in his absence. "He told me to anticipate a life physically without him," stated Winnie in a *People* magazine interview of February 1990, "that there would never be a normal situation where he would be head of the family. He told me this in great pain. I was completely shattered."

Nelson's prophecy came true in 1962, when he began a twenty-seven-year stint in prison. During that time, Winnie Mandela led the campaign for Mandela's release and visited him whenever she was allowed to do so. For years at a time Winnie Mandela was Mandela's sole contact with the outside world.

Winnie Mandela also continued to be active in the fight against apartheid, for which she was subjected to frequent harassment by the police. She was jailed for more than two years and was forced to live in a designated location for most of the twenty-seven years her husband was behind bars. To black South Africans, Winnie Mandela was considered the "mother of the nation."

Winnie was beside Mandela on February 11, 1990—the day he triumphantly strode out of prison as a free man. Around that time, however, they had been waging against the South African government. Mandela traveled throughout the nation espousing a nonviolent, negotiated settlement leading to full rights for all South Africans. He was welcomed by ecstatic crowds everywhere.

In July 1990 Mandela set off on an international speaking tour, to shore up support for his cause and to raise funds. Mandela thanked antiapartheid activists for their dedication to the struggle and urged foreign governments to continue economic sanctions against South Africa as long as apartheid remained in place.

In 1991, at a national gathering of the ANC, Mandela was elected to be the organization's president. Mandela then entered into talks with President deKlerk and leaders of other

Winnie Mandela. *Photograph by Juda Ngwenya. Reproduced by permission of Archive Photos.*

of being government informers. When she was convicted of kidnapping and fined in 1991, the ANC leadership decided that she was hurting their cause. In April 1992 Mandela announced that he and Winnie Mandela were ending their marriage. Winnie Mandela, however, continued to head the influential ANC women's league—a position that entitled her to a seat on the ANC leadership body. League members voted to remove Winnie Mandela as their leader in 1995. In 1997 she made an unsuccessful bid for the deputy presidency of the ANC.

Public opinion about Winnie Madikizela-Mandela is divided. Despite her fall into disfavor, she remains to many black South Africans a courageous leader.

allegations began to surface that Winnie had been involved in a conspiracy to kidnap and murder black youths accused

political parties. The outcome of the talks was the formation of a transitional legislature whose job it would be to draft a new constitution. Under the new constitution, all South Africans would have equal rights. In addition, multiparty elections, in which all South Africans could vote, were scheduled for 1994. Mandela and deKlerk were jointly awarded the 1993 Nobel Peace Prize for leading their nation down a nonviolent path toward democracy.

Wins presidency of South Africa

In the months leading up to the April 27, 1994, elections, Mandela committed all his energies to campaigning for president on the ANC ticket. On the day of the nation's first-

Mandela (right) meeting with U.S. president Bill Clinton in 1998 in Cape Town, South Africa. *Reproduced by permission of Archive Photos.*

ever multiparty election, people arrived at the polls early and formed lines that stretched for blocks. The experience was an emotional one for people who had waited their wholes lives to vote. The final tally showed that the seventy-five-year-old Mandela had won the race for presidency, with his ANC taking 62 percent of the vote.

In his acceptance speech the following week, Mandela stood beside Coretta Scott King, the wife of slain American civil rights leader **Martin Luther King, Jr.** (1929–1968; see entry). Echoing the sentiments of King, Mandela stated: "I stand before you filled with deep pride and joy—pride in the ordinary, humble people of this country. You have shown such a calm, patient determination to reclaim this country as your own. And joy that we can loudly proclaim from the rooftops: Free at last!"

Mandela's first priorities as president were improving the standard of living of the nation's long-oppressed black majority and promoting a national reconciliation. Neither task

Activists, Rebels, and Reformers

was easy in a nation plagued by poverty, crime, and racial animosity. During Mandela's tenure as president, his government built housing and provided running water for some three million people, increased the proportion of households with electricity from 31 percent to 63 percent, and constructed more than 350 health clinics in poor, rural areas (only 17 had existed in those places during the apartheid era).

Retires from presidency

As Mandela's eightieth birthday approached, South Africa experienced a bout of Mandela-mania. Newspapers ran full-page tributes to the aging leader, several parties were held in his honor (including one Mandela threw with one thousand orphans as his guests), and the post office printed a birthday greeting on millions of pieces of mail. Mandela surprised his supporters by announcing, on his birthday, that he had wed Graca Machel—widow of Mozambican independence leader and president **Samora Machel** (1933–1986; see entry).

Among the many birthday wishes Mandela received was the following from the guards who had watched over him at Pollsmoor Prison. "If we can stand tall and join hands we could rise above all doubts," they stated in an ad in a Cape Town newspaper. "Love is the only thing that will keep our country together, because the world has found a friend in you. May your ancestors smile upon you."

Mandela, deciding he would retire in 1999, announced he would not seek a second term of office. Instead, he threw his energies into the election campaign of ANC deputy president Thabo Mbeki. After Mbeki had won the election, Mandela retired to a villa in his birth village. Mandela's plans for the coming years included enjoying his hard-won freedom and the company of his wife, children, and grandchildren, as well as writing his memoirs.

Sources

Books

Benson, Mary. *Nelson Mandela: The Man and the Movement.* New York: W. W. Norton & Company, 1994.

Hoobler, Dorothy, and Thomas Hoobler. *Nelson and Winnie Mandela.* New York: Franklin Watts, 1987.

Mandela, Nelson. *Long Walk to Freedom: The Autobiography of Nelson Mandela*. Boston: Little, Brown, and Company, 1994.

Mandela, Nelson. *The Struggle Is My Life*. New York: Pathfinder, 1990.

"Nelson Mandela." *Contemporary Black Biography*. Vol. 14. Detroit: Gale Research, 1997.

Articles
"The Case Against Winnie." *Newsweek*. December 15, 1997: 39.

Cowell, Alan. "Mandela: Man, Legend and Symbol of Resistance." *New York Times*. September 5, 1985.

Daley, Suzanne. "For Mandela's 80th, Parties and Talk of a Wedding." *New York Times*. July 18, 1998.

Laufer, Stephen. "Truth and Apartheid." *The Nation*. January 12, 1998: 5+.

Leonard, Terry. "Mandela's Legacy: Reconciliation, Democracy Heralded." *Ann Arbor News*. June 1, 1999: A5.

Selsky, Andrew. "S. Africa Makes Progress since Mandela Release." *Ann Arbor News*. February 10, 2000: A8.

"Who Should Be the Person of the Century?" *Time*. December 20, 1999: 29.

Web Sites
"South Africa's First Post-Apartheid President." ABC News. [Online] Available www.abcnews.go.com/reference/bios/mandela.html (accessed February 5, 2000).

Selected Speeches, Statements and Writings of Nelson Mandela. African National Congress. [Online] Available http://www.anc.org.za/anc-docs/history/mandela/64–90/ (accessed February 5, 2000).

Horace Mann

Born May 4, 1796
Franklin, Massachusetts
Died August 2, 1859
Yellow Springs, Ohio

Educator, abolitionist, legislator,
and social reformer

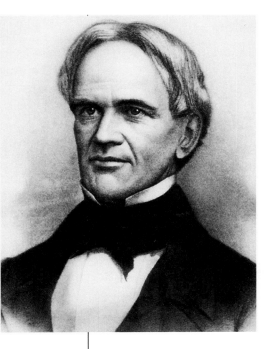

Horace Mann was born at a time when the public school system was in its infancy. Children like himself spent most of their time working instead of going to school. Youngsters who received an education were primarily those whose parents could afford to hire private tutors.

Mann believed that society had a duty to see that all children received a free, high-quality education. He made it his life's work to create a successful system of public schools in Massachusetts. He also established a network of "normal schools" for training teachers and helped develop standards for textbooks. As a member of the U.S. House of Representatives from 1858 to 1862, Mann fought for the abolition (outlawing) of slavery. In his final years he served as the first president of Antioch College in Yellow Springs, Ohio.

Values learning as a child

Horace Mann was born on May 4, 1796, on a farm outside of Franklin, Massachusetts. He was the fourth of five children born to Thomas and Rebecca Mann. As a boy, Mann worked hard on the family farm and attended school only ten

"Be ashamed to die until you have won some victory for humanity."

Horace Mann in Antioch College's 1859 graduation exercises.

Horace Mann.
Reproduced by permission of Archive Photos.

363

weeks out of the year. Mann and his siblings had to earn their own money to pay for their books. To do that, they worked in a small factory making straw hats. Mann supplemented his education by reading history books at the small Franklin Public Library.

When Mann was thirteen years old, his father died; his older brother Stephen drowned the next year. Mann was left to oversee the farm and to help care for his mother and younger sister. His greatest longing, however, was to go to college. Mann hired a tutor to teach him Latin and Greek (prerequisites for admission to college in those days) and prepared to take college entrance exams.

Attends Brown University

In 1816, when Mann was twenty years old, he was admitted to Brown University in Providence, Rhode Island. Because he had scored so high on his entrance exams he skipped his freshman year and began college as a sophomore. In college Mann was a star member of the debate team. He was elected president of his senior class and presented the graduation speech. In his speech he stated that "education should reach like a ladder from earth to heaven"—an ideal he worked to make a reality throughout his lifetime.

From law school to state legislature

Following college Mann worked for a law firm, then taught classes to first-year students at Brown University. He then enrolled in Litchfield Law School in Connecticut and graduated in 1823. After finishing law school, Mann was hired to work in a law firm in the small town of Dedham, Massachusetts.

Mann became famous throughout the region for his oratory skills and in 1827 was elected as a representative to the Massachusetts state legislature. His greatest accomplishment as a legislator was the passage of a bill mandating the construction of a state hospital for the mentally ill. Prior to that time, mentally ill people had been warehoused in jails, in terrible conditions of filth and cruelty. Mann saw to it that in the new state facility (the Worcester State Lunatic Hospital), which came to serve as a model for the rest of the United States, patients had comfortable quarters, clean surroundings, and humane treatment.

In 1829 Mann married Charlotte Messer, the youngest daughter of Brown University president Asa Messer. Three years later Charlotte Messer became ill and died. Mann had been deeply in love with her, and her death sent him into a long period of depression.

Begins crusade for public schools

After his wife's death Mann resigned his position on the state legislature and moved to Boston, Massachusetts, where he resumed practicing law. In 1834 Mann's colleagues convinced him to run for the state senate. Mann won the race in a landslide and became president of the governing body. In that capacity Mann first pushed for the reform of debtor laws. He felt it was immoral that thousands of citizens were incarcerated for being unable to repay small debts.

In 1837 Mann achieved his greatest legislative success: the passage of a law creating a state board of education. The purpose of the board was to overhaul Massachusetts's shameful public school system, in which students were educated only a few weeks every year in overcrowded, run-down buildings with unsatisfactory books and untrained teachers. Mann gave up his senate seat to become the first secretary of the board of education. He explained why he so valued education by saying, "Education, then, beyond all other devices of human origin, is the great equalizer of the conditions of men—the balance-wheel of the social machinery."

In the ten years that Mann served as secretary of the board of education, he was unstoppable in his crusade for school improvement. Mann collected information on the status of schools throughout the state by circulating written questionnaires and holding a series of local meetings. He presented the problems and proposed solutions in yearly reports to the state legislature. He also started a magazine called *Common School Journal*, published twice a month, in which he informed the public of reforms in the educational system.

Establishes guidelines for education

Mann's reports to the Massachusetts state legislature contained a number of recommendations that were eventually adopted by schools throughout the United States; indeed,

Mann's ideas still form the philosophical underpinning of today's public school system. Among Mann's suggestions were that education be free and compulsory (mandatory) for all children. He was an outspoken opponent of corporal (physical) punishment, stating that "to thwack a child over the head because he doesn't get his lesson, is about as wise as it would be to rap a watch with a hammer because it does not keep good time."

Mann also advocated that books used in schools be cost-free for students and held to certain standards of quality and content. He spoke out against the use of religious texts in schools, citing an 1827 law guaranteeing schools freedom from religious interference. He also began the tradition of placing libraries in schools and insisted that one hour each day be set aside for physical and health education.

Mann argued that, above all else, schools must be staffed by qualified teachers. Many of the teachers employed at the start of Mann's tenure as board of education secretary were poorly educated themselves and knew little about teaching methods. Mann initiated the establishment of "normal schools"—schools for the education of teachers. In 1839 the state's first normal school, funded by tax dollars, opened in Lexington, Massachusetts; two more normal schools were founded soon after in the towns of Barre and Bridgewater (both also in Massachusetts). Also under Mann's direction, two-week training institutes were offered throughout the state for teachers who could not afford the time or expense of attending a normal school. During Mann's tenure with the board of education, not only did teachers become better qualified but their salaries rose by 50 percent.

Studies European system of education

In 1844, twelve years after the death of his first wife, Mann married again. His second wife was a writer and educator named Mary Peabody. The couple eventually had three sons: Horace, Jr., born in 1844; George, born in 1846; and Benjamin, born in 1848.

Mann and Peabody traveled to Europe after their wedding, for a combined honeymoon and study tour of other nations' educational systems. The trip provided Mann with new ideas about how to improve teaching methods in Massachusetts schools. Upon their return, Mann and Peabody moved from their rented lodgings to a house in West Newton, outside of Boston.

Mann, who was ready to move on to new challenges, resigned his post as board of education secretary in 1848. In his final report he emphasized the need for students to learn critical thinking skills, and not just rote memorization. He also recommended that music be taught in schools.

Fights for abolition of slavery as U.S. Representative

In February 1848, shortly before he resigned as Massachusetts education secretary, Mann was sent to Washington, D.C. He had been selected to fill the vacancy in the U.S. House of Representatives created by the death of Representative John Quincy Adams (1767–1848; U.S. President from 1825–1829 and congressman from 1830–1848). In Congress Mann continued Adams's tradition of fierce opposition to slavery.

Mann won reelection to Congress on the Free Soil (antislavery party) ticket in 1850. The following year Mann unsuccessfully argued against the passage of the Fugitive Slave Law. (That law, which brought simmering tensions over slavery to a full boil, required federal marshals to arrest any black person accused of being a runaway slave. Arrests were made without warrant, solely on the basis of a slaveholder's assertion of ownership. The captured individual had no right to a jury trial or to give testimony in his or her own defense. Anyone caught helping a fugitive slave was subject to six months in jail and a $1 thousand fine.) In 1852 Mann was unseated by a proslavery candidate.

Helps launch Antioch College

Shortly before the 1852 congressional election, Mann had been invited to serve as the first president of Antioch College (today called Antioch University). Situated in Yellow Springs, Ohio, Antioch was different than any other institution of higher learning in the United States at that time because it accepted students of all races and both genders. At age fifty-six, Mann moved his family westward to begin this new adventure.

The Case of Fugitive-Slave Assistant Captain Drayton

In 1848, while serving in the U.S. House of Representatives, Mann directed the legal defense of two men charged with aiding runaway slaves: Daniel Drayton and Edward Sayres. Drayton, captain of the schooner *Pearl,* had been captured on the Potomac River outside of Washington, D.C., with a boatload of seventy runaway slaves. Drayton had been helping the slaves escape to the American North. (While it was not Drayton's first time helping slaves to escape, it was the first time he had been caught.) Drayton, along with the schooner's owner, Edward Sayres, was charged with "stealing and carrying away" slaves.

Mann vigorously defended the men in a summer-long trial. Mann claimed he was undertaking his legal action on behalf of the "whole colored race." In the biography *Horace Mann,* E. I. F. Williams described the trial: "Against oppressive summer heat, . . . with armed slaveholders in court daily, with hostile sympathizers with the slavery cause as a background, Mann had stood like the rock of Gibraltar for the black man's rights."

Drayton and Sayres were convicted at trial and sentenced to pay fines of $10 thousand each. Mann worked hard to have the men's convictions overturned. His appeals were partially victorious in that the fines were eventually reduced to $1 thousand each.

In October 1853, when the college opened, 150 students of all ages and walks of life began attending classes in the still unfinished buildings. Mann, who also taught courses in political science and philosophy, insisted that faculty bring creativity, enthusiasm, and a concern for humanity to the classroom. He wanted to ensure that Antioch graduates were not only schooled in academics but were also morally well-rounded.

As Mann soon discovered, however, Antioch's finances were in such terrible shape that it was difficult even to pay faculty salaries. Mann traveled extensively in an effort to raise funds for the floundering college. To make matters worse, within a few years of Antioch's establishment, the United States suffered an economic recession. In 1859 the institution, deeply in debt, was auctioned off. Fortunately, a group of wealthy supporters purchased the school and kept it running.

At the 1859 graduation ceremonies, Mann made what is regarded as his best speech. "In the battle in which you have engaged, against error and wrong," he said, "if ever repulsed or stricken down, may you always be solaced and cheered by the exulting cry of triumph over some abuse in Church or State, some vice or folly in society, some false opinion or cruelty or guilt which you have overcome! And I beseech you to treasure up in your hearts these my parting words: Be ashamed to die until you have won some victory for humanity."

Mann became ill shortly thereafter and died at his home in Yellow Springs on August 2, 1859, at the age of sixty-three.

Sources

Books

Lach, Edward L., Jr. "Mann, Horace." In *American National Biography*. Vol. 14. Edited by John A. Garraty and Mark C. Carnes. New York: Oxford University Press, 1999, pp. 424–27.

Lagemann, Ellen Condliffe. "Horace Mann." *The Reader's Companion to American History*. Boston: Houghton Miflin Co., 1991, p. 698.

Messerli, Jonathan. *Horace Mann: A Biography*. New York: Alfred A. Knopf, 1972.

Pierce, Edith Gray. *Horace Mann: Our Nation's First Educator*. Minneapolis: Lerner Publications Company, 1972.

Williams, E. I. F. *Horace Mann: Educational Statesman*. New York: MacMillan, 1937.

Karl Marx

Born May 5, 1818
Trier, Germany
Died March 14, 1883
London, England

Economic theorist, philosopher, and revolutionary; father of communist theory.

"Let the ruling classes tremble at a Communistic revolution. The proletarians have nothing to lose but their chains. They have a world to win. WORKING MEN OF ALL COUNTRIES, UNITE!"

final passage of The Communist Manifesto *by Karl Marx and Friedrich Engels.*

Karl Marx.
Reproduced by permission of Archive Photos.

Karl Marx was one of the most influential economic and political theorists of all time. His critique of capitalism (the economic system characterized by private or corporate ownership of factories, farms, and other means of production) and promotion of communism (the economic and social system based on the holding of all property in common) fell on the receptive ears of exploited urban workers in nineteenth-century Europe. In the years since Marx's death, many nations have undergone communist revolutions and attempted to put Marxism into practice. No nation, however, has achieved the final, ideal state of revolution described by Marx: that in which the central government withers away and the citizens direct their own destiny by producing goods for the benefit of all.

Christian upbringing

Marx was born on May 5, 1818, in Trier, Germany. At the time Trier was part of Prussia—a powerful military empire and monarchy of the seventeenth and eighteenth centuries (Prussia became part of the German empire in 1871). Marx's father, Heinrich Marx, was Jewish by birth but had disavowed his religion because of strong anti-Jewish sentiment at that time in Europe. The year before Karl was born, his father became part of the Evangelical Established Church.

Marx was baptized at the age of six and attended a Christian primary school. In high school Marx excelled at language and literature. (As an adult Marx was versed in French, Latin, Spanish, Italian, Dutch, Scandinavian, Russian, and English—as well as his native tongue, German). He also paid close attention to his religious studies and embraced Christianity. Marx finished high school at age seventeen, the youngest in his class.

Intellectual growth in college

Marx enrolled in the University of Bonn in 1835. His father, a lawyer, urged him to study law, but Marx majored in philosophy and literature. His goal was to become a poet and playwright. For Marx, his first year of college was a time of fervent studying, writing poetry, piling up debts, and drinking heavily (he even spent a day in jail for being drunk and disorderly). He also became secretly engaged to Jenny von Westphalen, a childhood friend and the daughter of a Prussian government official. As Marx devoted more time to socializing and less time to attending classes, his grades dropped.

After Marx's first year of college, his father, displeased with his son's performance, had Marx transferred to the University of Berlin—an institution known for its academic rigor. There Marx studied law and philosophy.

At that time there was an explosion of new ideas at the university; scholars were questioning religion, the universe, and the meaning of life. Central to the intellectual upheaval in Berlin was the philosophy of Georg Wilhelm Friedrich Hegel (1770–1831). Hegel employed the method of "dialectics" (from the Greek word "dialogue")—the evolution of thought produced by the clash of opposite ideas, or debate. In other words, one argument gives rise to a counterargument, and out of that exchange comes new ideas. Using dialecticism, Hegel attempted to justify the idea of God. He came to the conclusion that God exists insofar as humans created God, and that God dwells within humans. That assessment ran counter to the teachings of the church, which stated that God dwells in heaven and that God created humans.

Friedrich Engels: Marx's Life-Long Collaborator

Friedrich Engels was born in Prussia in 1820, the son of a wealthy textile manufacturer. As a student Engels was attracted to communism—the theory of social organization based on the holding of all property in common.

In 1842 Engels traveled to England to work as a business agent for his father. There he witnessed firsthand the miserable working and living conditions of those (including children) who toiled in the textile mills. Engels wrote an article about the exploitation of the English working class for the *German-French Annals,* then traveled to Paris, France, for a ten-day meeting of the publication. There Engels met a fellow contributor to the *Annals,* Karl Marx. Engels later wrote that by the end of the meeting he and Marx had reached "complete agreement on all theoretical matters."

Marx and Engels worked together closely until Marx's death in 1883. Engels, who always had more money than Marx, helped support the growing Marx family.

Friedrich Engels. *Public Domain*

Engels even wrote articles for Marx: an estimated one-third of all writings for which Marx was listed as author were actually penned by Engels.

Engels died in 1895. He never married or had children, but he had been involved in a twenty-year romantic relationship with an Irish factory worker named Mary Burns.

Weighs spiritual versus material realities

While Marx embraced Hegel's dialecticism, he rejected Hegel's idealism (the belief that reality is essentially spiritual, not physical). Marx was an adherent of materialism—the idea that the human condition is only affected by the material world, and that natural phenomena can only be explained through science (not religion or supernatural occurrences). Marx crafted a philosophy that was a blend of Hegelian and materialist thought, which he called "dialectical materialism." Whereas Hegel believed that a person's spirit could be free even if his or her body was in chains, Marx claimed that the only freedom that mattered was material. And he argued that under the capitalist system, in which a privileged rich minority exploits the masses of workers and deprives them of the fruits of their labor, the workers could never be free.

Marx and other members of the university community with progressive political leanings (called "left" Hegelians) interpreted Hegel's teachings to question the economic order of the nation, the belief system of the church, and the legitimacy of the Prussian monarchy. Some of Marx's professors espoused radical theories of religion and economics; they denied that Jesus had ever existed and asserted that factory workers would only be free under socialism (social and economic organization based on the control of the means of production by the community as a whole, rather than by wealthy individuals or corporations).

Writes and agitates in the name of communism

Marx completed his college courses and dissertation, and in 1841 he was awarded a doctorate degree. He then applied for a teaching position in philosophy at the University of Bonn, but the Prussian government (which had labeled Marx a rebel) interfered to make sure he did not receive the appointment.

In 1842 Marx began writing for a newspaper in Cologne, Germany, called *Rheinische Zeitung* ("Rhenish Gazette"). In his articles Marx criticized government policies—including the hoarding of wealth by the rulers and censorship (the act of suppressing writings and speech deemed objectionable). Marx's series of articles on the peasants of the Moselle district in Europe brought to light the suffering of poor people. In his editorial columns Marx advocated communism: the idea that there should be no private property. With Marx on board, the circulation of the paper soared, and that fall Marx was made editor-in-chief. In 1843, however, the government ordered the paper closed.

That June Marx married Jenny von Westphalen, over the objections of most of the bride's family members. The couple moved to Paris, then a center of socialism. Marx became involved in the revolutionary workers' movement and continued writing.

Two important events in Marx's professional life occurred over the next couple of years. First, Marx wrote an essay called "Toward the Critique of the Hegelian Philosophy of Right," published in the *German-French Annals*. In that piece he denounced religion as a symptom of humanity's deeper problems, and as a cause of those problems. "Religion is the sigh of the oppressed creature," wrote Marx." . . . It is the opium of the people. The abolition of religion as the illusory happiness of men, is a demand for their real happiness." The second significant event for Marx was meeting Friedrich Engels (1820–1895; see box). Engels, a writer who shared Marx's political outlook, became Marx's friend, colleague, and financial supporter for life.

Becomes a man without a country

In 1845 the French government, under pressure from the Prussian government, ordered Marx to leave the country. Marx moved to Brussels, Belgium. There he became involved in efforts to organize workers, but he was hampered by personal and political differences with other revolutionary leaders.

In 1848, during a worker uprising in Brussels, Marx was given twenty-four hours to leave the country. After a short stay in France, he returned to Cologne with Engels. There the pair founded a radical newspaper called the *New Rhenish Gazette*. In the pages of the paper Marx advocated that citizens resist the Prussian monarchy by refusing to pay taxes and taking up arms.

Marx was arrested and charged with inciting armed rebellion. In a famous trial Marx acted as his own lawyer. He turned the proceedings into an indictment of the Prussian monarchy by introducing evidence about the poor living conditions throughout the land. Although acquitted by the jury, Marx was expelled from the country by the government.

Marx next lived for short periods in Frankfurt (Germany) and Paris, and tried unsuccessfully to foment a workers' revolt in Germany. In August 1849 Marx arrived, with his family, in London. There Marx would spend the rest of his

The Communist Manifesto

In 1847 German immigrant workers in London formed a secret society called the Communist League. They summoned Marx and Engels to London to meet with them and then commissioned the pair to draft their political program. Marx and Engels took on the task, the result of which was the publication of a pamphlet in January 1848 called *The Communist Manifesto.*

"A specter is haunting Europe—the specter of communism," began the now-famous treatise. The pamphlet went on to state that workers "have no country" and owe allegiance only to their economic class. It defined the owners of the means of production (the bourgeoisie) as the oppressors throughout history and the urban poor, particularly factory workers (the proletariat), as the oppressed.

In the *Manifesto,* Marx and Engels advocated that workers come together in trade unions to intensify the conflict, until finally they would overthrow the bourgeoisie and establish a communist society. That society, according to Marx and Engels, would be characterized by the abolition of private property, a graduated income tax (where tax burden increases with income), free public schools, the abolition of child labor, and nationalization (putting in the hands of the state) of banks, communication, transportation, factories, and farmland.

The Communist Manifesto ended with the famous words: "Let the ruling classes tremble at a Communistic revolution. The proletarians have nothing to lose but their chains. They have a world to win. WORKING MEN OF ALL COUNTRIES, UNITE!"

days. Since England would not grant Marx citizenship, he remained a man without a country—or, in his words, "a citizen of the world."

Economic and personal hardships

Upon his arrival in London, Marx joined the Central Committee of the Communist League. His involvement with the group did not last long, however, because Marx clashed with other leaders over revolutionary strategies.

Throughout the 1850s Marx worked as a journalist. He sold some five hundred articles to the *New York Daily Tribune* (one-quarter of which were secretly authored by Engels), but the income from the articles was not enough to pay the Marx family bills. Even with financial assistance from Engels, who was working as a clerk, Marx and his family lived in dire poverty. Three of Marx's children died due to malnutrition and a lack of health care and medicine, and a baby was born dead. Marx was often unable to pay his rent, taxes, or debts. He could not afford heating fuel or shoes for his children. On more than one occasion Marx and his wife, Jenny, were forced to pawn their clothing. Jenny suffered from nervous breakdowns and physical illnesses.

Marx spent much of his time in the reading room of the British Museum, just a few blocks from his family's two-room flat. There he authored his first book on economic theory, *A Contribution to the Critique of Political Economy* (1859) and worked on his most prominent work, the three-volume *Capital*. (Only one volume of *Capital* was published during Marx's lifetime. Engels completed and published the other two volumes after Marx's death.)

Marx's own health also went into decline. Probably as a result of his poor diet and heavy smoking and drinking, Marx suffered from headaches, toothaches, boils, rheumatism, bronchitis, eye infections, and other afflictions.

Marx's final years

Marx's financial situation improved in the late 1860s, when he received inheritances from Jenny's family and greater contributions from Engels. He remained plagued by health problems and depression, however, and the pace of his writing slowed.

Marx was grief-stricken by the deaths of his wife in 1881 and his eldest daughter (only three of Marx's seven children survived to adulthood) the following year. On March 14, 1883, two months before his sixty-fifth birthday, Marx died of a lung abscess. He was buried in London's Highgate Cemetery; his grave is marked by a bust bearing his likeness. Marx's two surviving daughters later committed suicide: one in 1898 and the other in 1911.

Epilogue: The Russian Revolution

Marx lived his life in relative obscurity. Aside from serious scholars of economics and political science, few people had the patience to wade through Marx's complex and theoretical texts.

The words of Marx were first heard throughout the world in 1917, when revolutionary leader Vladimir Lenin (1870–1924; see box in **Rosa Luxemburg** entry) guided the communists to power in Russia. Lenin combined his own ideas with those of Marx to create Marxism-Leninism: the theory and practice of the dictatorship of the proletariat, and the ruling ideology of the communist state. Communism maintained its hold in the Soviet Union until the republic's dissolution in the early 1990s.

Since the Russian Revolution, Marxism has influenced social movements in many countries, including China, North Korea, North Vietnam, Cuba, Nicaragua, Algeria, Chile, Mexico, Hungary, Poland, Bolivia, Guatemala, Greece, and East Germany.

Banished from his native Germany, Marx died in London, England, and was buried there in Highgate Cemetery. This large headstone marks his grave. *Photograph by J. Gordon Melton. Reproduced by permission.*

Sources

Books

Brown, Archie, Michael Kaser, and Gerald S. Smith, eds. *The Cambridge Encyclopedia of Russia and the Former Soviet Union.* Cambridge, England: Cambridge University Press, 1994, pp. 333–37.

McLellan, David. *Karl Marx: His Life and Thought.* New York: Harper and Row, Publishers, 1973.

Payne, Robert. *Marx.* New York: Simon and Schuster, 1968.

Rius. *Marx for Beginners.* New York: Pathfinder Press, 1976.

Tucker, Robert C., ed. *The Marx-Engels Reader.* 2d ed. New York: W. W. Norton & Company, 1978.

Janet McCloud

Born March 30, 1934
Tulalip Reservation, Washington

Native American rights activist, women's rights activist, and spiritual leader

"We are the backbone of our communities—men are the jawbone."

Janet McCloud, from Messengers in the Wind.

Janet McCloud, a Tulalip/Nisqually Indian and mother of eight, has fought for Native American rights throughout her adult life. In the 1960s and 1970s McCloud was a leader in the movement for Native American fishing rights. She and her husband were arrested many times during fish-ins (protest in which participants fished in violation of state laws to assert their treaty rights).

McCloud joined the **American Indian Movement** (AIM; see entry), a militant Indian-rights organization, in the early 1970s. Later that decade McCloud founded Women of All Red Nations (WARN)—a women's group within AIM that worked to end domestic violence in Indian communities. McCloud, who has served as spokesperson for the Nisqually nation, operates a Native American spiritual center called Sapa Dawn on her property in northwestern Washington state.

Childhood plagued by violence

A direct descendent of Chief Seattle (1788–1866; signed treaty ceding land to white settlers in 1855; Seattle,

Washington, is believed to be named for him)), McCloud was born on the Tulalip Reservation in northwestern Washington state in 1934. During her childhood she was abused by her father and later her stepfather, both of whom were alcoholics. When McCloud's mother would go out of the house, leaving McCloud in charge of her three younger sisters and her cousins, her stepfather and other men with whom he had been drinking would sometimes sexually molest the children.

"When I was seven, I started organizing the cousins," stated McCloud in an interview in the 1995 book *Messengers of the Wind*. "We'd find a corner in the house, we'd make beds on the floor and would put all the little kids behind us. We'd get axes and knives, and when the drunks came, we'd go after them and run 'em out. So that was my first organizing."

McCloud's family would often be evicted from their home because her parents were unable to pay the rent. The family moved several times before McCloud and her siblings were placed in foster care. Even after she was safe from her stepfather's sexual assaults, McCloud was tormented by the memories of them, attempting suicide at the age of twelve.

McCloud did poorly in school and received little encouragement from her teachers. She dropped out of school in junior high. She says that her one academic strength, writing poetry, was crushed by a teacher and a principal who accused her of copying from a book three poems she had actually written herself.

Establishes self-sufficient lifestyle

McCloud's first marriage, which she entered into at an early age in order to get away from home, ended in divorce. She later married Don McCloud, a truck driver, and moved to Seattle, Washington. Within a few years the couple had purchased ten acres of land in Yelm, Washington (near Tacoma), and moved there to raise their family. The McClouds strove for self-sufficiency by hunting, fishing, growing their own food, and making their own clothing. They added rooms on to their log cabin to accommodate their growing family (they had eight children in all). The McClouds remained married for thirty-five years, until Don McCloud died of cancer.

McCloud explained her reasons for wanting to be self-sufficient in *Messengers of the Wind*: "If I have money, the power company takes it, the telephone company takes it, the tax people take it, the grocery stores take it," she stated." . . . So why should I accumulate money and make them richer? I grow my own food and dry it."

Leads the fishing rights struggle

In the mid-1960s, the fishing rights of the McClouds and other Native Americans in Washington's Puget Sound area came under attack (see box in this entry). Game wardens and other law enforcement officials tried to restrain Native Americans from fishing by beating and arresting them, ramming their fishing boats, and cutting their nets.

McCloud was among the Native Americans who organized a resistance to these tactics. She brought together Nisqually, Tulalip, and Puyallup Indians, whose livelihoods depended on fishing, to form The Survival of American Indians Association. McCloud purchased an old mimeograph machine and established a newspaper, called *Survival News,* to explain the Indian position in the fishing-rights battle.

McCloud and her husband were arrested several times during fish-ins in 1965. On at least two occasions state officials responded by ramming the McClouds's boat with high-powered speedboats. Don McCloud spent thirty days in jail after one fish-in. Following a lengthy battle, the Native Americans ultimately prevailed in their legal quest to fish without state interference (see below).

A victory for Indian fishing rights

McCloud and other Native American fishing-rights activists were handed a victory in 1974, with the decision in the landmark court case *United States v. Washington*. U.S. Judge George H. Boldt (1903-) of the Federal Court for the District of Washington State ruled that Native Americans were entitled to catch up to 50 percent of the fish in Puget Sound area—the traditional fishing region of the northwestern tribes at the time they signed treaties (the 1850s).

"Because the right of each Treaty Tribe to take anadromous [migrating from the ocean up a river to spawn; such as

The Roots of the Fishing Rights Battle

Beginning in the late 1800s, lawmakers in Washington state attempted to ban traditional Native American fishing practices. Law enforcement officials began arresting Native Americans who were fishing with nets or fishing at times outside of the established "fishing season." The officials, however, were acting in violation of treaties, signed in the 1850s, that exempted Native Americans from state-imposed fishing restrictions.

State lawmakers claimed they were trying to protect the dwindling salmon supply in the rivers that ran inland from Puget Sound; they blamed the salmon reduction on overfishing by Native Americans. Native Americans responded that the salmon loss was not caused by their traditional fishing, but by pollution of the river, the construction of dams, and commercial fishing operations—all caused by non-Indians.

In the mid-1960s tensions over Indian fishing rights in Washington's Puget Sound area came to a head. Game wardens and other law enforcement officials attempted to stop Native Americans from fishing by beating and arresting them, ramming their fishing boats, and cutting their nets. Native Americans, led by The Survival of American Indians Association, fought back. They were supported by the National Indian Youth Council—a group of young, mostly urban, Native Americans activists from Albuquerque, New Mexico—and Chicanos from the Seattle, Washington, organization El Centro de la Raza.

Beginning in 1964, activists held several "fish-ins" in northwestern Washington State. Hundreds of Native Americans activists were arrested during fish-ins; many were beaten by club-wielding police and game wardens. Some were shot at by white vigilante (citizen who takes criminal justice matters into her or his own hands) sports-fishermen. The Native Americans garnered national attention when actors Marlon Brando, Jane Fonda, and Dick Gregory joined the demonstrations.

salmon] fish arises from a treaty with the United States," Boldt wrote in his ruling, "that right is preserved and protected under the supreme law of the land, does not depend on State law, is distinct from rights or privileges held by others, and may not be qualified by any action of the State." Boldt's decision was twice upheld by the Supreme Court, which refused to hear appeals in the matter.

Participates in AIM's Longest Walk; Forms WARN

In the early 1970s McCloud joined the American Indian Movement (AIM). She served as a delegate to a national conference on prisons, held in Williamsburg, Virginia, in 1971. There she advocated that Native American prisoners be allowed to practice their traditional religions while incarcerated. While frowned upon by corrections officials in the 1970s, that practice is widely accepted today.

In 1978 McCloud participated in AIM's Longest Walk march from San Francisco, California, to Washington, D.C., in which activists demanded sovereignty (self-governance) for all Indian nations. Later that year McCloud (by that time known as Yet Si Blue, which means "a mother to all") and other women in AIM established their own organization, Women of All Red Nations. "We were tired of the sexist macho stuff we got from the men in AIM," stated McCloud in *Messengers of the Wind*. "We needed to do something for the women. We are the backbone of our communities—men are the jawbone."

Becomes spokesperson for Nisqually nation

In the 1980s McCloud received legal training so that she could write affidavits and briefs for Native American rights organizations. She also became the official spokesperson for the Nisqually nation. In that capacity she met with other members of the tribe to develop a plan for healing the physical and psychological ills of tribal members.

At the same time she got involved in countering anti-Indian discrimination in the school district of Yelm, Washington, on the outskirts of the Nisqually Reservation (the district where her eight children attended school). She also pushed for inclusion of outdoor education in the district's curriculum.

Another of McCloud's causes has been to oppose casinos on reservations. "The flood of casinos that plague our communities," wrote McCloud in a 1997 newsletter article, "have brought jobs and big money for a few and also crime and corruption. Far too many parents abandon their children every night and spend their food money at the casinos."

"We Are Women of All Nations"

Following are excerpts from this 1979 poem by Janet McCloud.

We are women of all earth nations
We live in cities and reservations
We sadly looked upon our past

We've survived the holocaust
Now a new one's coming fast
We must survive the final blast.

Oh, you women of all earth nations
mothers of future generations
Before Columbus came,
Peace and Plenty ruled this land
Children laughed
And all men sang
Women were beautiful
Healthy and sane.

Oh you women of all earth nations
Rise up now for your salvation.
Want and strife now rule this land
Children cry
And young men die
Women look at what you are
Is it what you want to be?

Oh you women of all earth nations
Better pray for your salvation
Five hundred years of misery
That we've struggled to be free
Now the end is very near
Hopes and visions very clear

Oh you women of all earth nations
The EARTH MOTHERS OF CREATION.

Focuses on spirituality at Sapa Dawn Center

McCloud's work in the last few decades has centered on her own ten-acre rural plot of land, on which she has established a spiritual center called Sapa Dawn. (Sapa is a native word for "grandfather.") There McCloud and her daughters hold traditional ceremonies, meetings of local Native American activists, and international women's gatherings. On the grounds of Sapa Dawn there is a garden, a smokehouse, a sweat lodge, a baseball field, and a playground. Tepees are set up and taken down as guests come and go.

"The elders have said this is a spiritual place," stated McCloud in a 1999 newspaper interview. "For over thirty years, we've used this land to teach our traditional ways. When all is going crazy . . . our people can come back to the center to find the calming effect; to reconnect with their spiritual self."

In 1985, at a five-day conference at Sapa Dawn, women from three hundred tribes formed the Indigenous Women's Network. The coalition continues to champion Native American rights around the world. Also in 1985 McCloud traveled to Nairobi, Kenya, where she was a delegate to the United Nations World Conference on Women. Throughout the 1980s and 1990s McCloud was in demand as a public speaker around the world, addressing such topics as Native American rights, spirituality, education, and world peace.

Spiritual counselor in her later years

As the century came to a close, McCloud was a grandmother of twenty-five (with an additional ten "adopted" grandchildren) and a great-grandmother of ten. She survived a stroke in 1997 and continued to serve as a spiritual counselor for Native American women. In *Messengers of the Wind* McCloud said:

> I don't call myself a healer. I do counseling. I feel I'm a caretaker of this place rather than its owner. We have a sweat lodge and ceremonial grounds in back. I was trained by elders, and now I' trying to pass on what I learned to the next generations. . . .
>
> One time, I was up in the mountains with a couple of friends and one said, 'If I die, I want to die in the mountains.' The other one said, 'When I die, I want to die by the ocean.' I was young then, and I thought, 'Well, I'd like to live in the mountains, I'd like to live by the ocean, but I'm not ready to die anyplace yet.'

Sources

Books

Josephy, Alvin M., Jr. *Now That the Buffalo's Gone: A Study of Today's American Indians.* New York: Alfred A. Knopf, 1982.

Katz, Jane, ed. *Messengers of the Wind: Native American Women Tell Their Life Stories.* New York: Ballantine Books, 1995.

White, Jonathan. *Talking on the Water: Conversations about Nature and Creativity.* San Francisco: Sierra Club Books, 1994.

Articles

Trahant, Mark N. "Native Leader Janet McCloud Finds Peace in Her Place, Her Victories, Her Family. It Has Taken Years to Get There." *Seattle Times.* July 4, 1999.

Web Sites

"Janet McCloud." Sapa Dawn. [Online] Available http://www.alphacdc.com /sapadawn/sapadawn.html (accessed February 16, 2000).

McCloud, Janet. "A Bird's Eye View of the Native Movement." (February 1977). [Online] Available http://www.alphacdc.com/sapadawn/natvmov.html (accessed February 16, 2000).

McCloud, Janet. "Message from Yet Si Blue (Janet McCloud), 1997." [Online] Available http://www.alphacdc.com/sapadawn/message.html (accessed February 16, 2000).

McCloud, Janet. "We are Women of All Nations . . ." (1979). [Online] Available http://www.alphacdc.com/sapadawn/wmn.-poem.html (accessed February 16, 2000).

Rigoberta Menchú

Born 1959
Chimel, El Quiché, Guatemala

Human rights activist and author

"The important thing is that what happened to me has happened to many other people too. My story is the story of all poor Guatemalans. My personal experience is the reality of a whole people."

Rigoberta Menchú in her autobiography,
I, Rigoberta Menchú

Rigoberta Menchú is a dedicated advocate for the human rights of indigenous (native) peoples of Latin America. Born to a peasant Mayan Indian family in the highlands of Guatemala, Menchú's childhood was marred by poverty and military-inflicted violence. She joined the movement for social justice and worked for change until driven from the country by death threats. After her exile to Mexico, Menchú continued her efforts for human rights.

In her 1983 autobiography, *I, Rigoberta Menchú*, Menchú brought the story of the suffering of indigenous Guatemalans to the world. In 1992 she was awarded the Nobel Peace Prize.

Childhood of poverty

Rigoberta Menchú was born in 1959 in the village of Chimel, in the remote highlands of the El Quiché province in Guatemala. Her family belonged to the Quiché group of Mayan Indians (Mayans—the original inhabitants of Guatemala and parts of Mexico—still constitute the majority population of Guatemala). Her father, Vincente Menchú, was an illiterate farmer who became a leader in the revolutionary movement. Her mother, Juana Tum, farmed and made clothing for the family.

Menchú's childhood was somewhat better than that of most other Mayan children, in that Menchú was able to attend elementary school. Like her eight brothers and sisters, Menchú also helped grow beans, corns, and potatoes on her family's small plot of land. The family lived in a stick house with a roof of palm fronds, with no electricity or running water.

To supplement their small income, the Menchú family spent part of each year harvesting coffee and cotton on large plantations on the Pacific coast. Even with their ceaseless work, the family could not get enough food; two of Menchú's brothers died of malnutrition at early ages.

Works as a maid

At the age of twelve, Menchú was hired out as a maid to a wealthy family in Guatemala City. There she discovered that, in contrast to the poverty that she had known all her life, there was a minority of nonindigenous people who possessed great wealth.

Menchú thus discovered what many other Mayans had already learned and were working to change. In the early 1970s Mayan activists joined with trade union members, peasants, and students to protest the unjust social system that upheld the interests of a tiny minority while condemning the rest of society (particularly Indians, who had no citizenship rights) to lives of virtual servitude.

(The oppression of the Mayan peoples had begun in 1524, when Spaniards conquered Guatemala and claimed the country's resources and labor for themselves. The Indians had for centuries endured their fate while quietly maintaining their traditions in their own villages. It was only in the aftermath of a U.S.-backed military coup in 1954 that conditions for indigenous people became unbearable and they began to resist their oppressors.)

Menchú began working on social-reform projects through the Catholic Church and a local women's committee. As an antigovernment guerrilla movement picked up steam in the late 1970s, social justice workers like Menchú found themselves increasingly the targets of police harassment.

Joins popular movement

In the late 1970s, following a series of armed-forces takeovers of indigenous people's lands and forced relocation of Indian communities, Menchú's father participated in the founding of the Peasant Unity Committee. Called the CUC for its name in Spanish, the committee was a union of agricultural workers.

Menchú joined the CUC herself in 1979. She traveled around the country, organizing people from various indigenous groups against the cruelty of the military (soldiers killed entire villages of Indians if they believed the villagers sympathized with guerrilla fighters) and the economic exploitation of the plantation owners (they paid indigenous workers very low wages). In 1980 Menchú was a leader of a sweeping farm-worker strike against the Pacific Coast plantations, and in May 1981 she coordinated large demonstrations by indigenous people in the capital, Guatemala City.

Family suffers at hands of military

Menchú's father, identified by the Guatemalan government as a leader of the CUC, was jailed numerous times. The armed forces sought to further punish Vincente Menchú by murdering his wife (she was tortured and raped before being killed) and one of his sons.

In January 1980, in an effort to draw international attention to the human rights abuses suffered by native Guatemalans, Vincente and others of the CUC had occupied the Spanish Embassy in Guatemala City. Police set fire to the building, burning alive the twenty-two people inside, including Vincente. After the building had been burned down, Rigoberta pulled the remains of her father from the wreckage. He had been burned so badly that he was nearly unrecognizable.

Seeks refuge in Mexico

After the embassy fire, it became clear to Menchú that she was the military's next target. She went into hiding and in 1981 fled to Chiapas, Mexico. There she was given refuge at the home of a Roman Catholic bishop.

Human Rights Abuses in Guatemala

In the 1970s and 1980s the Guatemalan military carried out one of the most brutal campaigns any nation has ever committed against its own people. It sought to stamp out the budding social-justice movement by killing activists, including peasants in the countryside, and politicians and union members in Guatemala City. They murdered people whom they accused of supporting the antigovernment rebel forces. In the year 1982 alone the military was responsible for over four hundred massacres, in which some one hundred thousand people were killed. Soldiers destroyed hundreds of Indian settlements and left nearly a million people homeless.

In the early 1980s, while supplying military aid to Guatemala, the administration of President Ronald Reagan (1911–; president 1981–89) turned a blind eye to human rights abuses. In response to reports by **Amnesty International** (AI; an international human-rights watchdog organization; see entry) documenting the terrible actions of the Guatemalan army, one U.S. State Department official called AI part of the "worldwide communist conspiracy" and accused AI of waging a "calculated program of disinformation."

In 1999 the United Nations Truth Commission (officially called the Historical Clarification Commission)—the body charged with researching crimes committed during Guatemala's civil war—found that about 93 percent of the political violence in Guatemala during the 1960s, 1970s, and 1980s was committed by the military (the rest was attributed to the guerrillas). The commission claimed that the military during that period had killed two hundred thousand people, most of them Mayan Indians, and had driven thousands of people into exile.

The 3,500-page report, called "Guatemala: Memory of Silence," also revealed, as the international human rights community had long suspected, that the United States government supported the Guatemalan military, even though U.S. intelligence sources knew of the human rights abuses being committed. After the report was issued, President Bill Clinton (1946–; president 1993–2001) expressed his regrets that the U.S. government had contributed to the suffering of the Guatemalan people.

From her new residence Menchú promoted human rights issues through the United National Working Group on Indigenous Populations and the International Indian Treaty Council. With the backing of those prestigious organizations,

Menchú gave public addresses and urged world leaders to pressure the Guatemalan government to stop its brutality against Indian peasants.

Autobiography becomes symbol of human rights struggle

In 1982, while in Paris, France, at the invitation of international solidarity organizations, Menchú (then twenty-three years old) met anthropologist Elizabeth Burgos-Debray. The two women decided to make a book of Menchú's life story. After spending one week together, in which Menchú spoke all about her life, Menchú returned to Mexico and Burgos-Debray began transcribing tapes. The product of that labor was a book, published in 1983, called *I, Rigoberta Menchú*. The book was very well received and drew international attention to the atrocities committed against Guatemala's indigenous population.

Receives Nobel Peace Prize

In 1992 Menchú received the Nobel Peace Prize for her work on behalf of social, political, and economic justice for Guatemalan Indians. She was the first Indian ever selected to receive the honor. "Today, Rigoberta Menchú stands out as a vivid symbol of peace and reconciliation across ethnic, cultural, and social dividing lines, in her own country, on the American continent and in the world," stated the Nobel Committee.

The committee's choice of Menchú for the award was somewhat controversial because of Menchú's ties to the antigovernment guerrilla force and her refusal to denounce violence as an acceptable means of evoking social change. Nonetheless, Menchú's prize was praised by the international human rights community as focusing the world's attention on the plight of indigenous peoples everywhere.

"Today we must fight for a better world, without poverty, without racism, with peace," stated Menchú upon accepting the Nobel Peace Prize. "I consider this prize not as an award to me personally, but rather as one of the greatest conquests in the struggle for peace, for human rights and for the rights of the indigenous people who . . . have been the victims of genocides, repression and discrimination."

With the prize money of $973,000, Menchú established a human rights foundation in honor of her father.

Becomes international human rights leader

Menchú's stature as a Nobel laureate provided her with a guarantee of safety in her homeland. Throughout the 1990s she has visited Guatemala several times to speak to peasant groups and to promote justice for indigenous peoples. In 1993 Menchú toured the United States and asked the U.S. government to grant temporary refugee status to Guatemalans who had fled military violence. That same year she traveled to Thailand to meet with exiles from Myanmar and to show her support for **Aung San Suu Kyi** (1945– ; see entry)—jailed independence leader of Myanmar and recipient of the 1991 Nobel Peace Prize.

Attends signing of Guatemala peace accord

In 1996, after a series of talks between the Guatemalan government and the rebel forces, the civil war was officially ended. Many people credit Menchú's work with bringing international pressure on the government to respect human rights. The agreement produced by the U.N.-mediated peace accords granted citizenship rights to Indians, established a system for redistributing land to landless peasants (2 percent of the population owned about 65 percent of the fertile land at the time the accord was signed), and provided for the return and resettling of refugees. It also included sweeping changes to the structure and mission of the military and police force.

"We who were born when the war was born have never experienced a Christmas without war," stated Menchú at the cease-fire signing ceremony. She cautioned, however, that both parties to the conflict would have to fully cooperate to prevent a repeat of the injustices that had plagued Guatemalan society for decades.

Publishes book on political problems in Latin America

In 1998 Menchú published her second book: *Rigoberta: La Nieta de los Mayas* (Rigoberta: The Granddaughter of the

Mayas). The book, written in Spanish, tells about Menchú's life since her first book written in 1983. In it Menchú recounts her life in exile, her involvement with the United Nations, and her views on the social, political, and economic problems (particularly the exploitation of indigenous people) of Latin America.

According to Gianni Mina, Menchú's collaborator on the new book, "This is the testimonial book of an indigenous Maya woman of the Quiché region of Guatemala who, having received the Nobel peace prize, reflects on the values of her civilization and of ours."

Discrepancies surface in Menchú's autobiography

In 1999 Menchú found herself at the center of a controversy regarding the veracity (truthfulness) of her autobiography. That year David Stoll, a professor of anthropology at Middlebury College in Vermont, authored a book titled *Rigoberta Menchú and the Story of All Poor Guatemalans*. Based on interviews he conducted with Menchú's relatives in Guatemala, Stoll was able to contradict a number of assertions made by Menchú. For instance, Stoll ascertained that Menchú had neither witnessed one brother die of starvation nor had she seen soldiers burn alive another of her brothers (both of which she had described in her autobiography). Stoll also countered Menchú's claim that she had no formal education, presenting evidence that she did, in fact, attend elementary school.

Menchú responded to the charges by stating that the inconsistencies were the result of translation errors, as well as miscommunication between herself and her editor (the person to whom Menchú told her story), Elisabeth Burgos-Debray.

The significance of these contradictions has been a matter of discussion among scholars and journalists. "The point of my book," stated Stoll in a 1999 interview, "is that . . . we have to put this appealing story she told into context because it is a story; it is just one version of events. He went on to say, "I think that the reason that Rigoberta denied that she had an education . . . is because her audience expects Indians to be barefoot, preliterate and traditional. . . . That isn't intentional racism, but it is a deeply ingrained prejudice that might deserve the label of racism."

Greg Grandin and Francisco Goldman, writing for *The Nation* on February 8, 1999, defended Menchú's autobiography from charges that its inaccuracies robbed it of its moral authority. "Her story was a call to conscience," they wrote, " . . . designed not to mislead but rather to capture our attention. It relied upon a classic . . . technique of pulling together different individual experiences into one character's heart-rending story."

"The undisputed facts of Menchú's story are horrible enough," Grandin and Goldman continued. "She *did* have two brothers who died of malnutrition at an early age; her mother and brother *were* kidnapped and killed by the army; and her father *was* burned alive."

Sources

Books

Menchú, Rigoberta. *I, Rigoberta Menchú: An Indian Woman in Guatemala.* New York: Verso, 1984.

Powers, Roger S., and William B. Vogele, eds. *Protest, Power, and Change: An Encyclopedia of Nonviolent Action from ACT-UP to Women's Suffrage.* New York: Garland Publishing, Inc., 1997, p. 318.

"Rigoberta Menchú." *Contemporary Heroes and Heroines.* Vol. 3. Edited by Terrie M. Rooney. Detroit: Gale Research, 1998.

Stoll, David. *Rigoberta Menchú and the Story of All Poor Guatemalans.* Boulder, CO: Westview Press, 1999.

Articles

Clarke, Kevin. "Digging up Old Bones." *U.S. Catholic.* June 1999: 39.

Dudley, Steven. "David Stoll on Rigoberta, Guerrillas, and Academics." (Interview.) *NACLA Report on the Americas.* March-April 1999: 8+.

Gaines, Judith. "Charismatic in Guatemala Effort, Menchú Eschews Violence for Peace Despite Killing of Three Family Members." *Boston Globe.* October 18, 1992: 14.

Grandin, Greg, and Francisco Goldman. "Bitter Fruit for Rigoberta." *The Nation.* February 8, 1999: 25–28.

Gugelberger, Georg M. "Remembering: The Post-Testimonio Memoirs of Rigoberta Menchú Tum." *Latin American Perspectives.* November 1998: 62+.

Holiday, David. "Reckoning in Guatemala." *The Nation.* March 22, 1999: 5.

Web Sites

Rigoberta Menchú Tum. Nobel Committee. [Online] Available http://www.nobel.se/laureates/peace-1992–1–bio.html (accessed February 9, 2000).

Index

Illustrations are marked by (ill.).

N

NAACP. *See* National Association for the Advancement of Colored People (NAACP)

NAAPID. *See* National African American Parent Involvement Day (NAAPID)

Nader, Ralph *2:* 320; *3:* 395 (ill.), **395–402**, 398 (ill.)

Naders Raiders *3:* 398 (ill.), 399–400

NAFTA. *See* North American Free Trade Agreement (NAFTA)

Naidu, Sorojini *2:* 199 (ill.)

NALC. *See* Negro American Labor Council (NALC)

Narrative of the Life of Frederick Douglass 1: 154–55

Nashville Student Movement *3:* 526

Nasrin, Taslima *3:* 403 (ill.), **403–10**

Nation of Islam (NOI) *2:* 345–48

National African American Parent Involvement Day (NAAPID) *1:* 164

National American Woman Suffrage Association (NAWSA) *1:* 5; *3:* 428, 521

National Association for the Advancement of Colored People (NAACP) *1:* 5, 49, 53, 159; *2:* 246, 260; *3:* 448, 479, 508, 524, 555, 577

National Black Women's Health Project *1:* 134

National Coalition on Racism in Sports and Media (NCRSM) *3:* 554

National Conference of Black Mayors (NCBM) *1:* 80, 86

National Conference of Social Work *1:* 5

National Congress of American Indians *3:* 555

National Consumers' League (NCL) *2:* 303

National Council of Negro Women *1:* 85; *3:* 464

National Farm Workers Association (NFWA) *1:* 98

National Federation of Charities and Corrections *1:* 5

National Guard *3:* 461–62

National League for Democracy (NLD) *3:* 543

National Opposition Union (UNO) *3:* 497

National Organization for Women (NOW) *2:* 271–72, 274 (ill.), 275; *3:* 555

National Political Caucus of Black Women *1:* 134

National Science Foundation *1:* 114

National Traffic and Motor Vehicle Safety Act (1966) *3:* 398

National Urban League *1:* 51; *3:* 448

National Woman's Party (NWP) *3:* 429

National Women's Hall of Fame *1:* 117

Nationalism *2:* 334

Native American fishing rights *1:* 31; *2:* 380–81

NAWSA. *See* National American Woman Suffrage Association (NAWSA)

Nazi Party *1:* 28

NCBM. *See* National Conference of Black Mayors (NCBM)

NCL. *See* National Consumers' League (NCL)

NCRSM. *See* National Coalition on Racism in Sports and Media (NCRSM)

Negro American Labor Council (NALC) *3:* 445, 448

Negt, Oskar *1:* 130

Nehrum, Jawaharial *3:* 469

Neighborhood Guild *1:* 4

Neighborhood Service Organization *1:* 162

NESAM. *See* Nucleus of Mozambican Students (NESAM)

New Left *1:* 14

"New Song," *1:* 20

New Rhenish Gazette 2: 374

New York Communist 3: 455

Newer Ideas of Peace 1: 7

Newcomb Cleveland Prize *1:* 114

Newton, Huey *1:* 72 (ill.), 73, 76

NFWA. *See* National Farm Workers Association (NFWA)